ESTRANGED BEHAVIOUR
The Underbelly of Society

Estranged Behaviour: The Underbelly of Society

by Tanita Ross-Cady

ISBN: 978-0-692-82250-0
Author Photo by William Thoren

Cover Design by Steven Church & William Thoren

Dedication

to all the ladies

who know

how to use their magic powers

Preface

*BARTENDERS*COCKTAIL SERVERS*HOSTESSES*

SECURITY GUARDS*DOORMEN*BARBACKS*

*BUSBOYS*WAITRESSES*WAITERS*DREAMERS*

*DRUNKS*SKUNKS*MONKS*PHILOSOPHERS*

*THE ABUSED*THE USED*

THE CRUDE AND THE LEWD *POSSUMS*RATS*

*THE LOSERS*THE REFINED*

*THE REGULARS*THE WICKED*

*CIRCUS MONKEYS*SNAKES*

*AND TO ALL WHO ARE AWAKE**

This book is for you.

This is a project that began because a coworker and I would have poetry text message battles when we couldn't handle the stress of the bar. We would lock ourselves in the women's restroom to hide. In numerous states of immense panic we would write each other these hilariously over the top, emotionally deranged poems. It gave us momentary peace in times of absolute mass hysteria.

The foreword and five poems were written by my dear friend, Killarney Tender. These stupid little poems began to give us a sense of relief in a place that we hated, but needed. As time went on these poems began to reveal very intimate insights about other aspects of our lives. Without her, this project would never have come to fruition.

Little did I know what this project would lead to.
I started to save the poems she and I would send to one another. After a while I started writing short stories about

other wacky events that transpired as well as previous experiences that stuck out to me from working in restaurants and nightclubs for the last ten years. The book transformed even more...

I experienced a dream one night that was so real and life-changing that I knew I had to include it within the book. Before I could completely understand where this story began to take me, it became the pinnacle of the entire project. Suddenly, it was very apparent to me I was meant to share these intense feelings of self-doubt, vulnerability and disappointment I had experienced in some realms of my life.

It has become one of the best healing experiences completing this book. Looking back at things now, I know everything has happened this way for a reason. This book is about a lot more than just puke, piss, and bar tales. It is also about dreams I was never able to pursue because of my own physical limitations and how that has affected my path.

I hope that these stories bring relief to those who are struggling to find the greater meanings, just know--

You are not alone.

What started out as a joke has now transformed into a three-year long project and I intend to keep taking these stories to the next level.

I met some extremely special people along the way who have inspired me to pursue this book in a way that I never had eyes for previously.

My intention is to get this book made into an animated movie or series.

I want to put this out there from the beginning.

I don't want to stop working at this until someone calls me with a proposal so I can see it on the big screens.

In the next year, you will see me all over the west coast at comedy clubs, open mic nights, on street corners, in parks, at coffee shops, in bars, restaurants, nightclubs, and all over the internet pushing the stories within these pages.

I have truly poured my heart into this book and at times it has felt very uncomfortable and revealing.

If you love it, support it. You will be directly supporting my dreams.

If you hate it, tell the world how vile you think it is so they will check it out as well.

I have an undying faith that it will all be worth it.

Stay tuned.

Acknowledgements

Thank you to the amazing cocktail servers, bartenders, and insane patrons who made these stories possible.

Thank you to all my kind regulars who always gave me good tips and were patient with me even when I was crying and snotting all over myself.

Thank you, Mama Wolf. I'll get you the Llama one day.

Thank you, my Saint Sue. I know you're going to read this book and wince, but I warned you! I'm sorry and I love you!

Thank you to my dear friend, Killarney Tender. You're the main reason why this book exists. You were the best teammate a girl could ever have in that battlezone. I promise that if something ever comes out of this book, I will always take care of you. You are one of the most inspiring women I have ever had the pleasure of being friends with.

Thank you to the Thoren family for making me believe this could be something larger than I ever envisioned. You sparked something inside of me that was not there before.

I will be forever grateful.

Contents

The Mask   *1*

Girls Night Out   *4*

Dearest Handicapped Restroom Stall   *8*

Le Cirque Maudit I of III   *9*

Parallels   *14*

Puppy Tongue Part I of II   *15*

Showtime by K. Tender   *20*

Mr. Lawyer   *21*

The Most Beautiful Girl I've Ever Seen   *24*

From Now Until Forever by K. Tender   *28*

I Left Her on the Battlefield   *29*

Twenty-Two   *30*

Hormonal Tonal Range   *34*

Le Cirque Maudit Part II of III   *35*

The Latina Sisters   *41*

Oil by K. Tender   *46*

The Jinn Race   *47*

Highschool Reunion   *51*

Easter Sunday   *59*

Please Go Home by K. Tender   *62*

A Middle-Aged Love Affair   *63*

Just Move More Quickly   *67*

An Expensive Hotel Steak   *68*

A Dinner For Lona   *70*

Puppy Tongue Part II of II   *72*

Through The Looking Glass   *78*

White Light by K. Tender   *83*

The Most Ugly Girl I've Ever Seen   *84*

Sharkfaces   *91*

The Wallflower   *92*

Le Cirque Maudit Part III of III   *97*

Formal Foreword

I will carry you with me in my apron
from now until forever.
Who knows--
Years from now we could reunite.
You: A famous writer--
pulled off on the side of the road
at a diner in the middle of nowhere
looking for a pineapple jalapeño turkey burger.
Me: Your wrinkly waitress
with long wispy strands of grey hair
and laugh lines from a weathered soul.
With breasts that sag, droop, and no longer keep their form.
Always with that giant flower behind my ear.
Until we meet again, my friend
-K. Tender

The Mask

I clock on at work and The Show begins.

The stage is mine.

It's my chance to make you fall for me.

It's my chance to get you to believe in me.

I want you to watch me.

Follow me closely.

For the remainder of the evening, I am your charming, submissive, orphic bartender.

I am your dancing Monkey.

I am Thee Almighty Ethanol Therapist.

I am the customer service ballerina with the nice butt that is slowly swaying in your direction.

I am the quiet diary you've been longing for.

I am the swift deliverer of preferred cocktails.

I am your favorite whipping post. I am your Martyr.

I'll laugh if you want me to. I'll cry if you want me to.

I want to know what makes you tick. I want to trick you.

I want to pick you apart and put you back together.

I wish to temporarily and miraculously solve all your complications with my spirits.

To be a successful bartender you must first be a convincing liar.

You must learn to fabricate elaborate stories efficiently and with bold conviction.

You must learn the way of the pseudo smile.

You must learn how to control your emotions.

You must know when to be silent.

You must learn to suppress the animal instinct to gouge out someone's eye.

You must bite down on the feisty tongue trapped inside your mouth.

You must learn quickly from your mistakes.

You mustn't panic. Never panic.

You must portray the illusion of serenity even when you are crumbling on the inside.

Why? Because the second you walk through the front door, it is no longer about you.

Forget about your jagged personal life for a little while.

Right now, it is about the grandeur show you're about to put on for some asshole who has never worked a restaurant job.

Why?

You have bills to pay and a dog to feed.

This is your chance to shine.

This is your chance to tell your story.

Do not ever take no for an answer.

Force them to remember you forever.

Force them to love you.

Give them your sweat.

Give them your blood.

This may be your one and only shot.

The potential to extract all the cash out of these entitled bar pigs is at the tip of your fingers, if you can learn to harness the ineffable magic powers of the sexually persuasive female verve.

Bartending will force you into endless horrifically bizarre scenarios that will test your patience for humanity.

You must be adaptable and treat every situation in a diametrical and unique manor.

No two people want the same service from you.

You will have a psychological break down at least ten times.

The hardest lesson is to simply let go.

Instead of getting offended about how poorly some people treat you sometimes--

Remind *yourself* how much they hate *themselves* and move on.

Do not waste a moment wondering why people act the way that they do, just look for solutions.

Always be confident and pleasant in the face of blatantly insecure ridicule.

Making the conscious decision to be kind and concise never gives anyone an opportunity to control your emotions.

When you own your emotions, you decide the outcome.

Remind yourself:

All of this acquired tolerance

will teach you valuable lessons

about life

and the universe

and all that bullshit.

Girls Night Out

The mood on the patio was harmonious and serene.

It wouldn't be that way for long.

People were quietly enjoying their cocktails while sitting next to the outdoor fire pit when all of the sudden--

Two robust, middle aged blonde women came barreling outside with an intensity closely resembling that of Canadian Musk Oxen.

Both of them had jeweled, ornate crosses embedded in the back of their white tank tops.

On Monday night Karaoke started at 9pm and these rookies were right on time.

For three hours my ears were ruthlessly tortured by stark, offensive renditions of Queen, Alanis Morissette, Depeche Mode, Britney Spears, Sir Mix A Lot, and Kid Rock. The women take a break from their off tuned Goose calling only to continue squawking amongst themselves at the end of the bar.

They suck down Cape Cods

I observe them from a distance

I smile and sashay around my customers

like the smoothest of operators

when out of the blue--

A man goes to pursue them.

What a brave, brave man. He sits to the far left.

He welcomes himself to their gruesome twosome and...

THE SHOW BEGINS.

He asks thee cliché questions:

"So do you ladies come here often?

So are you ladies single?

So have you ladies ever made out

with another girl before?"

The blonde on the far right begins to tell a story about herself, then mid-sentence, she pauses. She slowly leans over, puts her head underneath the bar and pukes. Not that much, only enough to fill a pint glass. She wipes her mouth with her arm and returns to the story she had been sharing. Both the brave man and the other blonde were so drunk and more interested in sharing stories about themselves that they didn't notice the shameless public upchuck. But apparently yes, from what I could hear, she had in fact made out with another girl before.

The brave man gets excited and begins to yell out,

"YOU SHOULD JUST DO IT!

THAT WOULD BE SO HOT!

YOU SHOULD MAKE OUT

RIGHT NOW!"

The brave man was cheering like he was at a Super Bowl party.

His eyes were bulging. He was spitting all over the place.

The two women looked at one another very seriously.

They began to shut their eyes and move in.

The decision had been made. It was happening.

They were definitely going to make out.

They smashed their faces together so hard that I could hear their teeth crack.

The bar had officially turned into a Sports Stadium and the fans were going bananas!

I looked down and saw the puddle of vomit splattered on the floor. I could see the Mint leafs from the Mojito floating in the retched concoction. She didn't keep that down for long.

The girls were really getting into it now.

They were straddling one another.

I had front row seats to a crappy softcore porno made for college boys. Is this what my life had come to?

Save me.

Somebody.

Anybody.

I turned my head for a split second and heard the echo of Iron barstools crashing against the floor--followed by the peculiar euphony of Wild Turkeys.

They had somehow flipped themselves half way into the fire pit. They were gobbling frantically as they caught aflame. Their feet were kicking aggressively above their heads. Their limbs were reaching out to anything within immediate grasp. Two men pulled them out of the fire by their ankles. I grabbed the two large water pitchers sitting on top of the bar and dowsed them. One of the pitchers was filled with ice only.

I watched in slow motion at their facial expressions as I hurled chunks of frozen water straight into their gullets.

The ice bounced arduously off their chins and foreheads.

The gobbling turned to gurgling as the glaciated aqua face fucked them back to reality.

It was at this point these women realized that it was just another Monday and they were no longer in their prime.

Their sun was setting, slowly but surely.

The horizon led to an unavoidable, encroaching darkness that would eventually swallow them whole.

The entire bar stopped and formed a tight circle around the drenched wenches.

They had chicken in their teeth and bleu cheese in their hair.

"Don't you go to the Church right up the street by the high-school?" a young guy from the crowd yelled.

One of the women rolled over into the puked up Mojito as she stood up and ran out of the bar. The other woman called her husband to come and pick her up. When her husband arrived, he got out of the car and walked in through the front door. He saw his wife sitting there wobbling around like an old bowl of jello and he grimaced. He turned and walked back out the front door and she chased after him.

"I'm sorry Steve! It'll never happen again! This time I swear it! I promise you. I love you Steve! You know that I love you Steve!" She screamed at him.

I looked out the front window and saw two little girls inside of his car.

He got in the car and locked the doors; the woman hit the windows from the outside and continued yelling.

"I fucking love you Steve! I FUCKING LOVE YOU!"

He drove out of the parking lot--

leaving her behind.

This wouldn't be the last time.

Dearest Handicapped Restroom Stall

Thank you for your loyal silence.

You have seen my worst sides.

Sometimes how I act isn't very endearing.

As I sit on the toilet and avoid all the hungry single men who wish to suck me dry--

I begin to think about my life.

I think about riding horses on the beach in slow motion.

I think about picking up all the dog shit I've neglected.

When I can no longer endure the pains of the cruel, fast paced floor--

I crawl to you.

Cross eyed--pulling myself out of the blackhole of bad tip face twitching.

Within the four walls of your stall I can have my moment of solitude.

I won't cry tonight.

I won't leave defeated.

I will win the battle.

I will go out there and smile.

I will put on the Mask and be pretty.

Le Cirque Maudit I of III

"Do you still do all of that Circus stuff?" He asked me.

"Of course." I lied through my teeth.

I was in denial.

I had packed up and moved to a fantasy world.

I wasn't coming back anytime soon.

"Where do you go to learn something like that?" He went on.

I paused to think of a credible fabrication.

"I just kind of practice on my own now." I was dishonest.

I was ashamed of the words my tongue allowed. I hadn't practiced in over a year. The Circus was my calling. I had found my purpose in life and I was finally happy.

"I just think that's the coolest thing in the world. I look at pictures of you dangling twenty feet in the air hanging in that giant piece of Silk and it's so--out of this world" He was mesmerized.

I was willing to risk my life for something I loved so dearly. The Aerial Silks was the most dangerous, dazzling and splendiferous entity I have ever given myself to. One wrong move and you are dead. There is no fucking up allowed. It was something he could never understand. This particular Circus Apparatus had me enchanted in a dream like state. It was a state in which I never wanted to wake up from.

It is an indescribable sensation that cannot be explained with capricious, common expressions and words.

I felt my eyes glaze over as I thought about my atrocious fate. I was SIX months away from going on tour around America with a traveling Aerialist group when one day I started to experience painful cramping in my hands.

As the weeks went by it became serious. Anytime I went to throw my body weight around I felt like my fingers were going to break off of my palms. I took two weeks off. It was the longest two weeks of my life. I hissed and moaned the entire time like a spoiled brat.

I wanted to feel the wind in my hair.

I wanted to soar high above the trees and all the commonality.

I was hoping my hands would get better but they just got worse instead. I tried to fight it but my weaknesses were as clear as daylight itself. My teacher told me she thought that I should go to a specialist. I made an appointment and as they brought out the X-rays of my hands, they looked nervous to tell me the results.

The doctor told me there were pills, specialty therapies, surgeries, and other routes I could take but I would not be able to continue the Aerial Silks, Lyra Hoop, or any other kind of Circus Apparatus if I wanted to recover from my injuries. My hands were weak, and they were going to get even worse in time.

I was defective. I was 24 with the bone quality of a 55-year-old woman they told me. I tried to look at the bright side but it was absent. My dreams were ripped from my grasp. I stopped going to my classes. I stopped talking to my teachers.

I slept for days. The days turned into months. The tears knew no end. I would lay in bed hoping that time would elude me until an eventual end revealed itself. My future seemed arbitrary. I constantly had dreams where I was performing on a magnificent stage. The audience was in awe of my alluring presence. I'd wake up emptied of any emotion that had previously echoed.

This was not how my life was supposed to be.

Flash forward a year and I had moved back to Southern California.

I got a bartending gig down at the old neighborhood watering hole. I grew up in that area but I had moved away for four years to try and find a part of myself that I had left behind. I ended up feeling more lost than when I had started. I would see kids I went to high school with and they would ask me:

"DO YOU STILL DO CIRCUS STUFF?"

"CAN YOU SHOW ME HOW TO DO CIRCUS STUFF?"

"WHERE DID YOU LEARN THAT STUFF?"

"HAVE YOU EVER THOUGHT OF AUDITIONING FOR THE CIRCUS AND ALL THAT STUFF?"

I tried to lock it down and not get upset. I would excuse myself to the bathroom to weep pathetically. All I wanted was to join The Circus and be free from a senseless, average life where I go to a 9 to 5 job which I loathe.

Now--I was a bartender instead of a performance artist.

I wished so badly to reclaim my place amongst the legendary constellations and instead I was a liquorwench.

I slowly started finding my place in society again. My unattainable desires took their designated place on the back burner. They began to fade into a deeper part of my conscience and whispered to me less and less. I buried those dreams in a place I hoped no one would find them. I made friends with some of the girls I worked with and finally, a sense of normalcy began to creep back into my life. I took a liking to one girl specifically.

Sunny had recently moved to the West coast from New Jersey. She wanted to start a new life for herself. If anyone understood that, I did. She never spoke about her life in too much detail; I assumed it had been tough for her. I found out she did Circus Apparatus Arts as well. She proposed that I come to meet her in the park so that we could dangle in the sky together.

I told Sunny I would be there at high noon.

I felt my epidermis light on fire.

I yearned to be high up off of the dirt.

I yearned to be high with the birds.

I yearned to be high with the twinkling stars.

I yearned to be high with those ever-evolving planets--

Even if it were only for a brief moment.

I knew I wasn't supposed to but I couldn't say no. It had been a year. I reasoned with myself that my hands had in fact healed a little bit. The next day I sped as quickly as I could to the park.

I arrived at the park and there she was--

Faultlessly tangled in the royal blue 40 ft. silks.

She stretched and elongated her slim figure.

She would climb to the top,

slowly wrap up her body with the smooth fabric,

and then drop herself within an inch of the ground.

Death was her pacifier.

They began to dance.

I was enamored by her grace.

There was something too perfect about the way she moved.

All the attempts I had made to bury my feelings in the last year rose quickly to the surface and flooded me like the Spring Nile. Why did my hands have to quit on me? I was so inexpressibly jealous. I was so infuriated at the cards I was dealt.

I felt like retching up all of my envy so I walked away to have
a moment to myself.

I looked into the distance--

There was a carnival going on right down the street.

I could see The Mary Go Round

and The Ferris Wheel.

I took some deep breaths--

tried to regain some false form of composure--

and...

*That's when **He** appeared.*

Out of nowhere--

an enormous, muscular, chilling Man

with a grizzly beard

and twirling eyebrows.

He floated 3 feet above the ground.

I knew that I had seen Him before--

somewhere

deep

inside of my dreams.

I looked into His insensate, black eyes

and something

inhuman

looked right back at me.

Parallels

I put on my headphones

then I stretch my extremities

and for a couple of moments

I am at the center of this Universe

I kick high to the thermosphere

I dip low to the soil

I swing my body like I live in a little house on the prairie

I can feel that there is no separation from myself and everything else

I am empathetic

I am kindhearted to others

I envision a parallel dimension in which the hills are alive

and I don't have to bring sides of ranch to rude pieces of shit

I wake to a concrete reality

where the absence of rational thought

guides me towards my second psychotic break this week

The milk is expired

and the sob story is ancient history

That's when I put on my headphones

and for a couple of moments

I am at the center of the Universe

Puppy Tongue Part I of II

He sat at the corner of the bar.

He was staring at me.

It didn't matter how much time would pass.

I'd be running all over the place and every time I looked up, his body was faced in my direction.

His attention was zoned in on my every move.

After hours of being quietly studied from a distance I broke the barrier.

"What's your name?" I asked him.

He had a calm, breezeless demeanor.

"My name is Beau--but you can call me Puppy Tongue."

"Puppy Tongue? That's an interesting nickname."

"It's a factual nickname." He told me.

"Factual?"

"Yes, I have the softest tongue in the world and I lap it--like a puppy." He licked the air.

It wasn't every day that you meet a man so proud of such a nickname.

His bloodshot, venerable eyes were so blue that they cut through me.

He looked like he had been left out in the sun all of his life.

He was a very short man.

He had jagged, sharp teeth that crowded his massive mouth.

I could feel the air around him thicken. It was those eyes.

Those eyes were something else.

I had met plenty of creepy old men in the past.

Puppy Tongue was different. I was going to get inside this man's head. He had stories I wanted to hear.

Needed to hear.

I decided that I would win this creepy, epigrammatic battle of wits at any cost. He happened to stumble into the right bar tonight.

> *So often you see older men uttering sexual comments*
>
> > *to younger girls.*
>
> *The girls become intimidated and the old farts*
>
> > *always get the last laugh.*
>
> *Rarely does a little lady spit venom back and leave*
>
> > *a grown man disjointed.*

Oh yes, today he was going to get challenged by someone equally as uncanny. If he wanted to play this flirtatious, predatorial game of psychotic perversion, I was going to play it right back and smash him like a bug.

"Tell me about yourself, Puppy Tongue." I encouraged him.

His eyes grew large and he became excited.

He twisted me with that brakeless stare.

He leaned in and smiled a big, shark like smile.

"Are you scared of me?" He asked me quietly.

"No." I smiled back.

"Why not?" He got closer.

"If you try anything funny, I'll scream and every man in this bar will tear you apart." I whispered into his ear.

"I like your spirit. I knew there was something special about you." He went on. "I'm an author. I write erotic short stories and novels. I am going to write a story about you. But I need to know who you are first. So, we're not going to talk about me right now, we're going to talk about you."

"What do you want to know about me, Puppy Tongue?" I fed into it.

"I want to know about your first love." He asked me.

"I fell in love for the first time when I was fourteen years old. I used to run away from home all the time. No one was ever supervising me, so I went where ever I wanted, with whoever I wanted. I had gotten expelled from school and ended up at an establishment for the kids who had been kicked out of their districts too. It was a slew of riotous teenagers beating the shit out of each other, using copious amounts of drugs, and screwing in the bathrooms when none of the teachers were watching. I got caught up hanging out with all of the older boys at school. That's how we met. We would spend hours on the phone talking about anything and everything, and sometimes we just sat there in silence. My mother would drop me off at school and I would ditch my classes and walk down to his house. It was only one month after I turned fourteen when we had sex for the first time. I never realized how abnormal all of it was. How was I supposed to know any better? I was fourteen. I thought it was cool that an older boy wanted me."

"How old was he?" He asked.

"Twenty-one." I answered.

"Tell me more." He gave me his undivided attention.

"After a while, I never went home, I spent all of my time over at his place. We didn't go out in public too much. He was my teacher, my lover, my best friend, and my father. He was very intelligent and manipulative. He could convince me of anything. I believed everything he said; he was my Charles Manson and I liked it that way." I looked longingly into Puppy Tongue's deviant eyes and gave him the frenetic performance he had wanted all along, "I ate his words and laid in his bed for years upon years. I swear that's all I did for most of my teenage life was lay in his bed. Even though I knew something was strange within my heart, I didn't want to leave. I just wanted to be his. He was a magician. When he'd call I'd come. I always came back. He'd be in my dreams; he'd be in my nightmares. No matter what terrible events transpired, I always found myself back at his house, wanting him to want me."

I reached up

and touched my heart

as if something

was trying to escape

from my chest

and gave him

the most poignant expression

I could muster up.

"How long did this go on for?" His voice was eager.

"Fourteen years." I counted on my fingers.

"So essentially all of your romantic life?" He asked.

"That's right." I smiled coyly.

"How do you feel about all of it now?" He pulled a cigar out of his coat pocket and cut the tip off.

"I feel good about it. I have grown up to be an observer. I learned things early on that some women don't understand until later in life, or sometimes never at all. I am a lot more clever than I look. I am more emotionally intuitive than most women. I am near impossible to control. I am thankful for the awareness that I have now, in a strange way he gave me magic powers of my own. I can read people very well, even from across a room and it's all because of him." I lit his cigar for him.

"I've dated world class women-" He told me. "-movie stars, senators, Olympic gymnasts, doctors, Princeton lawyers and let me tell you something--they were all bitches. Your energy is--sensational. I can feel it burning me right now as we speak. May I touch your face?" He asked me.

"Sure."

He slowly reached towards my forehead with his index until he made contact with my skin. He trailed his finger down my cheek until he came down to my chin.

"And you have such soft skin too..." He sighed.

"Thank you." I replied.

His eyes were still ripping me in half.

"I am going to leave." He said, "I am feeling quite inspired. More inspired than I have felt in years! I'm going to go home and get wasted fucking drunk and write the most fantastic erotic story about you tonight!!"

I started to giggle.

"You don't believe me, do you? That's fine. I will be back. The next time you see me, I will have a special gift for you."

He kissed my hand
and walked out the back door
into the shadow of nightfall.

Showtime by K. Tender

Thirteen years down the drain.

I am nothing more than that broken green tile--

in that godforsaken sickening women's restroom.

Who knew what I was getting myself into?

I dry my tears and apply the mascara.

Two minutes until showtime. Good lord I look worn.

I will continue to smile through the pain.

Too poor to buy new pants.

Too poor to buy new underwear.

I check the zipper twice.

Who needs 'em anyway? I mutter to myself.

Needs. Not wants.

I pray these old work pants don't tear during my shift.

I am fat and unrecognizable to myself.

The patrons love me because they are fat too, broken and

disfigured by life.

I am like a mirror to them.

They see parts and pieces of themselves in my reflection

and I somehow remind them of home.

One day we will die here.

Maybe we already have.

Mr. Lawyer

Scott is the most interesting Lawyer I have ever met.

He looks like a handsome male version of Ellen DeGeneres.

He always dresses in custom handmade Gucci suits.

Today he is wearing an all-white suit with a baby blue dress shirt underneath. He looks like a Scarface Ken Doll.

"I can heal people--" he says confidently.

He is cross eyed.

He is drooling.

I am choking on his Aqua Di Gio.

"I just put my hands on people and they begin to weep." He closes his eyes.

"Wow Scott, I had no idea you had a gift like that. Would you like another margarita?" I ask.

"Yes, I would please."

"Ok."

"When I know someone needs to be healed, I will touch them and begin to pray hard. Depending upon what kind of demons are within them, I will pray silently or scream as loud as it takes. It exhausts me; I cry and roll around in my bed for days afterwards like I am fighting a flu." He closes the menu and reaches for the Margarita.

"I think the chicken club sounds good today." He says.

"Absolutely. No problem. Would you like another margarita, Scott?"

"Yes."

"Ok."

"So this one time I was leaving a bar downtown, I was hammered. I was feeling really angry with the world. It had been a terrible week and I thought to myself: Why does Satan think he is so BADASS!? Seriously though, have you ever asked yourself that question, young lady? He can cause all this pain--he can ruin everyone's life and hide behind the scenes like some coward piece of shit! What a God damn joke! He thinks he's so almighty. I will not tolerate such blatant fucking disrespect!" He screams.

"Here's your chicken club Scott--is there anything else I can get for you?"

"A side of thousand island, please." He asks politely.

"Ok."

"So I'm standing in the back alleyway and look up at the sky." He continues, "I raise my fists into the air and yell out, SATAN! IF YOU ARE SO BADASS--COME OUT AND FIGHT ME! I CHALLENGE YOU! MAN TO MAN! I WILL TAKE YOU DOWN! I WANT TO SEE IF YOU ARE REALLY AS BAD AS EVERYONE SAYS YOU ARE! SHOW YOURSELF YOU GIANT PUSSY!"

"Would you like another margarita, Scott?"

"Yes."

"Ok."

"I stood there for a couple of minutes and nothing was happening." He went on, "So I finally give up and start walking back to my car. All of the sudden--three large Marines come down the alley and *somehow* they are more drunk than I am. One of the men made a comment under his breath about how I looked like a fag. So I shouted back: COCK SUCKERS! I BET YOU HAVE SMALL COCKS! YOU PROBABLY SUCK EACH OTHERS FUCKING COCKS TOO! That's when they surrounded me. I woke up in the emergency room the following day with my four front teeth missing. I had to get reconstructive surgery on my nose and cheekbone. My ribs were broken and my organs were bruised. I pissed blood for 3 days and my balls swelled up like Grapefruits. Satan really messed me up! I challenged Satan and got the tar beaten out of me. That bastard won."

"Scott, would you like a box for the other half of that chicken club?"

"Yes."

"I guess the lesson of this story is not to call out Satan, Scott." I handed him a to-go box.

"He just caught me off guard. I'm going to challenge him again one day when I'm more prepared. Now that I know how he fights--next time, I'll be ready for him."

The most Beautiful Girl I've ever seen

It was a cold November evening

but that didn't stop the young club girls

from wearing the shortest dresses possible.

Thursday nights I was the door cashier. This meant I was one of the first smiling faces people would see before they would get inebriated and start dancing on the tables. It was a more diverse crowd than any other I had witnessed. Rich people. Poor people. The everyday girls who were being dragged out by their desperate friends who had just been broken up with by their boyfriends.

There were glamorous flamboyant gay men, and women who looked like men. There were the George Clooney and Diane Lane types. People reeking of recently smoked weed followed. Thursday was a Top 40 hit night. This meant that there would undoubtedly be lots of Army fights and twerk battles.

Working at a bar is so different from partying at one. When one remains sober and watches the alcohol induced makeout sessions from the side lines night after night, it changes you. The lights come on at 2am. You see all the big, nasty sweat stains and the lazy eyes. You see the bad decisions, the mistakes and the regrets.

A group of women came in and they were dressed in tiny, scant cocktail dresses. Their faces were painted up like Ronald McDonald's whores. The leader of their insecure, fertile Wolf pack was a perfect Asian/African American girl. She was absolutely stunning. I watched the look on the men's faces as she entered the room and they were all cockeyed and drooling. She was about to get eaten alive and dry humped half to death. She had an enchanting, bouncy ass that resembled two large scoops of chocolate ice cream.

Her eyes were shaped like almonds. Her hair was thick, straight, and stretched down to her hips.

She was irresistible.

She was a man's dream.

She was a woman's nightmare.

She was the most beautiful girl I've ever seen.

Suddenly the first girl fight broke out.

"Ma'am! Your breasts are out!" Security yelled.

"I'LL KILL YOU BITCH!" One girl shrieked.

"STOP SWINGING! YOUR BREASTS ARE OUT!" Security tried again.

Two security guards were holding back two women.

The second girl's dress was ripped in the front and her entire tit was violently flopping around as she tried to punch her opponent.

The first girl's blood and eyeliner was smeared all over her face.

"YOU FUCKED ENRIQUE! HOW COULD YOU DO THAT TO ME?!" The first one said.

"HE LOVED ME FIRST!" The second one started to cry. "STOP!! SWINGING!!" Security yelled.

The two women kicked each other like Kangaroos.

Shoes were flying and earrings were being ripped out.

The first girl was not wearing any panties and her muffpie was fully visible for everyone to see.

The tuft between her legs was covered in glitter.

"Last Call for alcohol!" The DJ said over the loud rap music.

My boss came running over to me in a state of panic.

"THE WOMEN'S RESTROOM IS OVERFLOWING WITH SHIT! THERE IS LITERALLY SHIT AND WATER ALL OVER THE FLOOR! GET ALL OF THE GIRLS OUT OF THE BATHROOM SO THAT WE CAN SEND MARK IN THERE TO UNCLOG THE TOILET!"

I rushed down the busy corridor to the women's restroom. I pushed the door open and there were four women staring back at me. The whole bathroom smelled like fermented asparagus and backed up drain pipes.

"EVERYONE NEEDS TO GET OUT OF THE BATH-ROOM! AS YOU CAN SEE WE ARE EXPERIENCING SOME OVERFLOW!" I started to say.

They all started talking at once.

"--I have to pee really badly--"

"--I have to wash my hands really quickly--"

"--Our friend isn't feeling good--"

"EVERYONE GET THE FUCK OUT OF THE BATHROOM RIGHT NOW!!!" I yelled.

Two of the girls high tailed out of the bathroom.

"Please, our friend isn't feeling well. She may barf."

That's when she turned around. It was the leader of the Wolf pack. The most beautiful girl I had ever seen was now clearly blacked out. She was so drunk she looked straight through my soul into a galaxy far, far away. I knew that look. She was definitely going to throw up. She pushed open the stall door. She flopped down onto the flooded, shit water floor with her perfect bare asscheeks and started throwing up. Her long, gorgeous hair was now inside the toilet as she hurled up all of the Lemon Drop Shots. She was missing one shoe.

Her hands were flat palmed onto the ground for balance as she fed the toilet the remnants of her stomach lining.

"Go in there and take care of her! We need to fix this toilet!"

I pushed her friends into the stall and closed it shut.

Mark entered the restroom with the Plunger ready for war.

The beautiful girl's one golden pump heel was sticking out of the bottom of the stall like the defeated Wicked Witch of the East.

This was a Rite of Passage.

Clubs bring out the worst in some people.

Mark began to plunge the filthy porcelain hole like a true bloodthirsty Viking.

Mark was working that toilet with such rugged force he began to sweat profusely.

He groaned intensely--

like he was in the midst of having his way with a woman when suddenly he cried out:

"AAAAAAAAAARRRRRRRRRRRRRRRGGG!!!!!!!!!"

A title wave erupted into the air.

Brown, putrid, murky liquid went spraying all over the walls.

Mark victoriously raised the Plunger above his head like a battle axe.

He had won the war.

He stuck his hand into the toilet bowl and pulled out a purple and black weave.

It resembled a skunk.

Mark breathed heavily as he held up his fresh Kill.

From Now Until Forever by Killarney Tender

You are a ghost now.

But I still see you.

I take you with me during my shifts.

I see your reflection in the restroom mirror.

I feel you when I make my pre-shift tea.

I think about you when those bastards taunt me with their smartass remarks.

"Wow! Four kids?" They say.

"All from the same dad?" They ask.

Fuck you. I think to myself.

Fuck you.

I cringe inside but force a smile.

Time for more lipstick.

Good God it's only one hour into my shift.

I am already contemplating ditching my diet and fueling my sorry ass in the darkness with some nachos.

Extra salt.

I know you will meet me there.

Please don't ever take your soul from this place.

I just might not make it tonight.

I left her on the Battlefield

As I wait for an imaginary moment of inner peace
    to come upon me
        I think about how I let her down--
I should have mustered up the energy to help her
    but the davenport beckoned my weight upon it
My jaw shakes when I envision
    thirty people all eager for their checks--
        all separate--
        all cash
The nerves in my stomach begin to eat me alive--
    when I remember all of the empty glasses
        begging to be retrieved
            by a prompt and agile female warrior
I scream like the spinach dip
    after it has been left in the microwave for too long
        Will she ever forgive me?
        I left her on the battlefield
Trays were flying
    Chicken tenders blazing
    in the background

Twenty-Two

Four young girls came waltzing in and sat at the bar.

They were giggling their tits off.

One of them was toting around a large bundle of balloons with the words 'HAPPY 22ND BIRTHDAY!' blasted across the front. They hit me with thee question:

"CAN YOU RECOMMEND SOMETHING GOOD AND SWEET, BUT NOT TOO SWEET, BUT REALLY STRONG, AND CHEAP?"

There was a long pause. We stared at each other. I blinked rapidly and in excess. I whipped up a drink that would surely induce a large, unforgivable sugar hangover. I made sure to top this drink off with an excessive amount of whipped cream. The other girls all ordered AMF's. Jesus Christ. Really? I don't ask questions. I just make the drinks.

Within an hour everyone had caught wind that it was this young girl's birthday.

This was an excuse for the regulars to get more drunk than they usually did.

The single men were buying them shots. Everyone wanted to socialize with them.

These men pretended that they were interested in the topics of discussion such as the perfect contouring techniques and whether high waisted shorts were hot or not.

The men nodded their heads and agreed with whatever they believed would get them into the high waisted shorts.

All of the sudden--
An Old Man kicked open the back door.

"I HEARD WE HAVE A BIRTHDAY GIRL IN THE HOUSE!!!!" He screamed.

His fist was raised above his head.

He was swinging his beer with such gusto it was spilling all over the floor.

His bulbous gut hung out the bottom of his Nascar t-shirt. His stringy grey hair was so long that it reached his nipples.

"I NEED TO GIVE SOME WORDS OF ADVICE TO THE BIRTHDAY GIRL!" He insisted.

As he spoke he inhaled his hair and choked on it.

He coughed up green mucus and it expelled all over the Birthday Girl's silver tiara.

He slammed his jumbo beer down onto the bar and the contents violently erupted like Mt. St. Helen.

He began to give the young ladies his advice.

"I HAVE GONE DEEPER, BEEN WETTER, AND CAME UP MORE SATISFIED THAN ANY MAN YOU WILL EVER MEET! THE SEA HAS GIVEN ME A HAPPINESS NO WOMAN COULD EVER GIVE ME! I HAVE BEEN MARRIED THREE TIMES! ALL OF THESE SOUL SUCKING WOMEN LEFT ME WITH ABSOLUTELY NOTHING!! I WAS IN THE NAVY FOR 20 YEARS GIRLS LISTEN CLOSELY!"

Everyone was silent. He continued.

"IT SEEMS IN MY PERSONAL EXPERIENCE, YOU WOMEN NEVER KNOW WHAT YOU REALLY WANT! FIGURE OUT WHAT YOU WANT BEFORE YOU INVOLVE YOURSELF WITH A MAN! MEN ARE STUPID! MEN WILL ASSUME YOU KNOW WHAT IN THE HELL YOU ARE TALKING ABOUT! YOU WOMEN ARE WAY TOO EMOTIONAL! HOLY SHIT! IF YOU LEARNED TO CONTROL YOUR EMOTIONS YOU COULD RULE THE ENTIRE WORLD!"

He was dribbling spit down his chin but never broke his seriousness. He let out a long, muffled, wet fart that went on for almost six-seconds.

"NEVER--AND I MEAN NEVER--TRY TO CHANGE A MAN!

"Patrick, I think we should probably go--" His friend tried to drag him off.

"A MAN IS WHAT HE IS! A MAN CANNOT BE CHANGED! YOU HAVE NO BUSINESS TRYING TO CHANGE A MAN! HE WILL NEVER IN ONE MILLION YEARS CHANGE FOR A GOD DAMN WOMAN! INFACT HE WILL RESENT YOU IF YOU TRY TO CHANGE HIM!"

"-Patrick, seriously, they're trying to enjoy a girls night out-"

"SEE THAT'S THE THING YOU DEGENERATE! THESE FINE YOUNG WOMEN ARE GOING TO BE WIVES ONE DAY AND THEY NEED TO KNOW WHAT IT TAKES TO PLEASURE A MAN AND KEEP HIM SATISFIED!!!LADIES! LADIES...YOU MUST LEARN HOW TO MAKE A DAMN GOOD SANDWICH. LEARN HOW TO GIVE A MEAN, MEAN BLOWJOB. LEARN TO BE INDEPENDENT AND THE MEN WILL FLOCK TO YOU LIKE FLIES ON SHIT! IGNORE A MAN AND HE WILL MISS YOU. IF YOU CONSTANTLY HANG ALL OVER THEM AND NEVER GIVE THEM ANY SPACE THEY WILL EVENTUALLY GET BORED OF YOU AND FUCK YOUR BEST FRIEND!!"

The girls wanted to gasp but they held their mouths shut.

The fart was hot boxing them; they were in the gas chamber of putrid bunghole waiting for deliverance.

Their eyes all gunned back and forth at one another.

They were already getting overly emotional thinking about who was going to fuck whose boyfriend and who was going to make the best sandwich.

"I KNOW FROM PERSONAL EXPERIENCE! LEARN HOW TO MAKE A DELICIOUS SANDWICH AND EVERYTHING WILL BE OKAY! I PROMISE YOU!"

The old man leaned down to give the birthday girl a hug and instead he lost his balance.

He flopped onto the ground like a salmon.

He got up.

He tried again.

Hormonal Tonal Range

They're all looking right through me as if I'm already gone.

I am a fossil compared to the life I once possessed.

The Sun brings droplets of sweat to my feral brow.

I am the mere memory of a girl--

who could weave her visions with Golden Thread.

I come and go like a ghost and no one notices how transparent I've become.

Is this it for me?

I crave something more.

I need something else.

I can't do this any longer.

I'm putting in my two weeks today.

Gibberish leaves my quivering lip.

I didn't mean it.

I need relief.

I want the warmth of inspiration--

Not the constipation of spinach dip while I flip.

Frustration debilitates my common sense.

I dive into the Ben and Jerry's.

My period should be here any day now.

Le Cirque Maudit II of III

This man was levitating.

He hovered 4 feet above the ground.

I couldn't move my body no matter how hard I tried.

Sunny started running away from the man and suddenly she fell to the ground. It looked as if an invisible fishing line had been cast around her ankle. She was being dragged back across the dirt with such force her legs were being ripped apart by the gravel. She was being pulled back by something. I couldn't see what. She finally came to a stop.

She lay there on the ground panting like a dog.

A dust cloud rose up and surrounded the three of us.

My heart was thumping in my ears.

"I HAVE FINALLY FOUND YOU SOFIA! YOU THOUGHT YOU COULD RUN AWAY FROM ME?! WE MADE A DEAL! YOU SIGNED THE CONTRACT!!"

The bearded man had a thick Russian accent.

"I DON'T WANT TO BE A PART OF YOUR DAMNED CIRCUS ANYMORE!" Sunny screamed at him.

"SOFFIIIIAAAAAAAAAAAAAAAAAAAAAAAAAA!!!!!!!!

YOU KNEW THE CONDITIONS OF THE CONTRACT!!!!

DO YOU KNOW HOW MUCH TIME I HAVE WASTED SEARCHING FOR YOU??"

The two yelled back and forth at each other.

"Who is this guy, Sunny?" I asked.

"He works for The Big Man--and my name isn't Sunny--It's Sofia."

I was growing more confused by the minute.

Sofia was Sunny's real name?

What was this Damned Circus?

How was this man levitating?

"I didn't move here from New Jersey--I've been running away for 100 years trying to escape this sociopath!" Sofia uttered.

"SOFIAAAAAAAAA!!! I GAVE YOU EVERYTHING YOU WANTED AND THIS IS HOW YOU REPAY ME?? YOU WANTED HELP AND SO I HELPED YOU!! YOU NEVER HAD ENOUGH TALENT TO MAKE IT ON YOUR OWN!! EVEN WITH ALL OF THE POWER I'VE GIVEN YOU, YOU ARE STILL SO WEAK!! IT MAKES ME SICK!!"

He spat on the ground.

She started to cry.

"YOU KNOW I HATE IT WHEN WOMEN CRY!!"

The dust began to settle and I could finally see again.

Sofia stood up.

I was terrified to see how badly her legs were cut up,

but as I looked closer--

The wounds were gone.

It was impossible.

I had just seen gashes that were oozing dark red blood only moments prior to the dust cloud lifting around us. I was positive I would have to take her to the hospital to tend to her injuries. I examined her legs thoroughly and it didn't make any sense. There was not even one tiny scratch that was visible.

It was as if all of the blood had just disappeared in the dust cloud.

"YOU WILL PAY FOR THIS SOFIA! DO YOU UNDER-STAND ME?"

"Yes." She said.

"Yes, *what*?" He yelled at her. She frowned.

"I said, yes *what*?"

"Yes, *Master*." She caved.

I went to hug her and when I looked at her face—

My skin started to crawl.

The pretty girl was gone.
Her physiognomy had changed.

She was now a decrepit old woman.

She had black eyes and moth-eaten skin.

"Now you see her for whom she truly is."

The Russian Man said to me.

"Sofia has never been trustworthy. You can always depend on her to be undependable." He went on.

I felt like I was in a science fiction novel.

"I believe we have gotten off on the wrong foot." He continued. "My name is Mkhail."

He reappeared behind me and pulled my hair into a pony tail.

"You look stunning with all of this hair pulled back. Wear it up more often. Has anyone ever told you that you have the face of a star?" He whispered into my ear.

"How did you get behind me so fast?" I asked him.

"I have been watching you for years." He told me.

I looked over to see if Sofia was okay.

She was surrounded by five gorgeous young women who also looked strangely familiar to me.

"Don't worry about Sofia. Those girls belong to us and they will not hurt her."

"Belong to us?" I asked.

"Yes. They all signed The Contract." He exclaimed.

"What are you talking about?"

I blinked my eyes and reappeared somewhere else.

I was now sitting at an old wooden table inside of a colossal Circus Tent.

It was nighttime and there were hundreds of white candles placed on the surrounding tables and fixtures.

Mkhail and I were alone together.

He beguilingly smoked a strong odoured cigar.

"Everyone has something that they want." He started.

"Sofia and the other five girls all had something that they wanted desperately. They were willing to sign The Contract for the opportunity of a lifetime, and for The Glory."

Sofia and another beautiful blonde girl walked into the Tent. Sofia was holding a large feathered pen and the blonde was holding a tattered, yellowish folded piece of paper. The blonde girl had a backpack on that had an adorable baby boy sleeping peacefully in it. I looked at the baby and couldn't help but smile because he was unusually precious.

"I would never sign away my soul. I don't care about The Glory enough to give up the rights of what should always remain free. My soul is untamable."

"You don't literally sign your soul away. That's the whole point of these Contracts is that it's a mutually beneficial partnership." Mkhail leaned back in his chair.

"What are you talking about?"

"I'll tell you more about that part later. Right now, I want to tell you more about your friend Sunny, who is actually Sofia. One hundred years ago I found Sofia in Portland, Oregon. She was an uncoordinated, bumbling, amateur performer but her heart was truly in it. She loved to dance but she was just so damn clumsy. She had no natural born talent. Sofia fell down the stairs one night and broke her neck, leaving her paralyzed. I watched as Sofia cried night after night wishing that her life had been different. I approached her with The Contract one night. We started traveling all over the world doing big shows, she had never been happier! And *this* little blonde number right over here!!" He pointed to the girl with the baby on her back.

"Her name is Penny. Penny was a drug addict with dreams of being in Cirque Du Soleil. Her boyfriend was beating the living day lights out of her. She found out she was pregnant and kept using drugs even though she knew it was wrong. The boyfriend inevitably found out that she was carrying a child and he beat her so badly he sent her into labor. The baby survived but was born prematurely and was horribly deformed from all the drug use."

"But the baby looks fine." I said

He rolled his eyes at me--

and then he snapped his fingers.

Penny turned into a wrinkled, frail, old woman and the baby on her back became hideously disfigured.

"She signed The Contract, *that's the only reason* that the baby looks healthy. She wanted to save her baby and escape her abusive boyfriend so she signed The Contract."

He snapped his fingers again.

Penny was youthful and the baby was cute once more.

"There is no way you will get away with all of this. The family members of these woman and the police will be searching for them."

"Haha! That is where you are wrong. I know that you are still trying to cling to the last shreds of your *extremely* limited view of reality, but the fact of the matter is, once you agree to sign The Contract you never existed at all. Poof. Gone. It is as if you were never born. The memories of you are erased from the minds of everyone that you encountered. Nobody knows who you are or that you're missing. Life goes on as if you were never there to begin with."

"How is that possible?"

"Anything is possible, my dear girl."

He puffed on his cigar.

The Latina Sisters

"I weel hava Belvedere an soda wit THREE LEMONS, por favor."

A thick Spanish accent rolled down her tongue and out of her mouth.

"My name ees Esperanza, don't ju forget eet sweetie."

Her lips were glossy and plush.

Her skin resembled an enticing hue of brown sugar.

Her hair was black like a Raven.

Her eyes were dark and confident.

She was about 5'1 with a thin waistline and a fat ass.

"I weel jus hava water for now, hunny."

Sitting next to the first gorgeous Latina woman was a second, equally as stunning Latina woman.

"An my name ees Rosalinda. I might wan sum dessert een a leettle beet, I'm jus fantasizing for right now."

She winked at me.

Their eyes moved across the patio--

Their demeanors were animalistic.

They were on the hunt, for something--or someone.

They were searching for prey to sink their teeth into.

"Ju see that guy over there?" They asked me.

They pointed to a tall, muscular Caucasian man wearing a button-down, long sleeve jean shirt.

"Can ju tell heem to come over here an seet weeth us please? We wanna talk to heem. Tel heem we hava question."

I walked over to the other side of the bar where the tall white man was sitting.

"Do you see those two hot ass Mexican girls over there?" I asked him.

He smiled and nodded his head yes.

He seemed dopey and impressionable.

He was one of those men that was too handsome for his own good. He never had to be funny, intelligent or have a fraction of a personality to attract women because he was over six feet tall with blonde hair, blue eyes, and a set of flawless teeth.

"They have a question for you. Go talk to them." I told him.

He got up quickly without saying a word and joined the ladies at their table.

"Hola sexy man! What ees jur name?" The girls asked him.

They giggled and pointed their tits at him.

"Hi ladies!" He said in a thick southern accent. "My name is Lowell."

The girl's grins grew so large that they looked like hyenas.

"I AM ESPERRANZAA! AN THEES EES MY SEESTER ROSALEENDA!"

"Nice to meet you Esperanza and Rosalita." He said.

"EES NOT, ROSALEETA! EES ROSA-LEEENDA!"

"Oh, I'm sorry, uh, Rosalinda." He scratched his head.

"A Southern boy, huh? Where are ju from Southern boy?"

"El Paso, Texas." He answered.

"That ees sooo sexy, so are ju lika cowboy or what?"

"No... Actually, I'm in the marine core. "

I walked around the building to catch a breath of fresh air.

The security guard came over and informed me that the young gentleman celebrating his twenty-first birthday was now throwing up in the bathroom like a pregnant woman.

"Which one?" I asked.

There were three separate twenty-first birthdays occurring that night. God save us all.

"It's the ginger wearing the fedora, purple dress shirt and the black suspenders."

"I'll go let his party know."

When I walked back to the patio I noticed the Southern Gentleman was no longer sitting with the Latina Girls.

All that was left was his empty beer glass.

I went and asked them, "Where did he go?"

Both the ladies had their arms crossed and looked down at the floor.

"He got scared." They looked disappointed.

"But ees okay, we got hees phone number and we gonna call heem all tha time until he hangout weet us."

They cackled harder than was necessary.

"Thas right he can't get away from us now, mmm mmm nooo girl." They were already plotting their attack.

Sometime later, the girls vacated.

As the night was coming to an end, I ran into Lowell.

"Those girls told me that they scared you off." I said playfully.

"Hail yea they scared me off! Those chicks were freakin' nuts!"

"What do you mean? They seemed nice."

"Nice? Dude! They said they were gonna rape me and shit."

"THEY WERE TWO HOT LATINA GIRLS!" His friends yelled at him.

"HOW DARE YOU RUN AWAY FROM TWO HOT GIRLS WHO THREATEN TO RAPE YOU!" They couldn't understand it.

"No man--y'all don't get it. They started showing me pictures of dildos and stuff!"

"It's not like they were gonna put them up your butt, man!" His friend tried to reason.

"See! That's what happened next! They started showing me pictures of dildos in asses!"

"Whose ass?" I asked.

"Their ass!" Lowell belted.

"One of the girls asses!?" His friends slobbered.

"Yeah man!"

"But who was sticking the dildo in her ass!?" I asked.

"Her sister was!" Lowell replied.

"The sisters were dildo-ing each other's asses!?" His friends went cross-eyed.

"Yeah, man! One of them showed me a bunch of crazy ass pictures of them banging each other's butts with all sorts of different contraptions I have never seen before. Man, I just moved here from Texas three months ago, I have never had any kind of woman show me *anything* like that. I have been scarred. You cannot unsee that kind of stuff! I'm a Marine. I've seen all sorts of nasty shit but they seriously scared me."

Half of his friends understood why he ran away so quickly.

The other half of his friends

were enraged

and confused

about how he could pass up

such a strange and exciting opportunity.

It was finally 2 a.m. and everyone had left the building.

The bar was silent and peaceful.

The cleaning crew had arrived to make this sticky and soiled
place look presentable, once more.

Lowell The Southern Gentleman

walked out the back gate

and left his full beer on one of the tables.

Such a waste of six dollars.

Oil by Killarney Tender

Life will cut us until we bleed my friend

But when you see you are bleeding--

at least you know you are still alive

Like a stale cheese quesadilla--

I find myself waiting

I appear to be collected and still--

although on the inside I am hardening quickly

Oily and cold

Bland and old

I am no longer fooling anyone

When will I break free from this tortilla?

*So I'm driving away with lessons learned--my truck packed
full of baking dishes that were once filled with lovingly cooked
food, surfboards and clothes.*

I'm trying to believe in the beauty of choices

There is no such thing as wasted love

And we cannot lie to ourselves

The Jinn Race

An older, thick blonde woman accompanied a man to the bar. He was walking very slowly with a wooden cane. She helped him get onto the stool.

He unbuttoned his dark grey shirt and revealed a tattoo on his right collarbone. The tattoo was an image of two small black holes with blood dripping out and running down his chest.

"I got this to always remember what happened." He said to me.

"Who shot you?" I asked.

"I didn't get shot--" He went on, "These are bite marks."

"What?"

"These demonic, smoke-like midgets would enter my home every night right before dawn and feed on me." He looked into my eyes.

"Excuse me?"

"I was very depressed for a long time. When they started to come and suck my blood, I actually began to regain some happiness in my life. I started looking forward to something." He told me without breaking seriousness.

"Okay, tell me more." I played along.

"Well, first off, these creatures speak telepathically. After a while I could hear them talking to one another across my bedroom, across my house and then eventually inside of my head. I could hear them laughing and making jokes all night long. I felt like they were allowing me into their secret realm. They began to talk to me as well. I really felt like I was a part of something. They started asking me to leave the door unlocked for them, so I did. Right before the sun would come up, every morning around the same time they'd hover up the staircase and come straight into my room."

"Hover?"

"Yes. These fuckers can hover, they are very quick. I think they may be capable of teleporting but I'm not entirely sure. Haven't been actually able to catch them mid-teleportation. All I know is that I would be laying in my bed patiently waiting for them to come. All of the sudden these floating clouds of black smoke would appear, I'd blink my eyes and they'd already be attached to me."

"And then what would happen?" I asked.

"They would begin to suck on me. They'd suck on my fingertips, they'd suck on my elbows, and they'd suck on the back of my head, that always hurt the worst. They knew exactly what they were doing because right before I would lose too much blood and get too weak, they would stop."

"Teleporting blood sucking midgets? Really?"

"Yes. Like I said before, I was very depressed. These blood sucking midgets brought me some kind of happiness. But happiness or not--I am no one's fucking sheep!"

"What do you mean by that?" I didn't understand.

"I was good enough to feed off of, but not good enough for anything else. After a while when they'd come to suck on me, and I would scream out loud, CHANGE ME! MAKE ME ONE OF YOU! I WANT TO BE ONE OF YOU! But they never changed me. It was very frustrating."

"How long did this go on for?" I asked.

"Hmm--about four months I would say." He looked up and to the right.

"FOUR MONTHS?" I shouted at him.

"Yeah. About four or four and a half months."

"Where do you live at?" I inquired.

"Oh, right down the street." He pointed to La Cresta.

"Sorry, if I may ask, why do you think they chose you?"

"Well, maybe because I'm 54 and I've never been with a woman before."

"--Never?" I raised my eyebrows.

"Well, I lied. I was with one woman one time--but I used a condom. I've never had unprotected sex with a woman." He told me.

The woman he came with started fidgeting in her stool and was beginning to look slightly uncomfortable.

"I mean that makes sense. You have mostly untainted virgin blood." I giggled.

"I got sick of being their sheep and I began to fight back when they would come at night." He said.

"How did that go over for you?"

"At first it was pretty bad, but I got a couple of punches in. But see, that's the thing about these creatures. When you touch them--they feel plasmatic. Almost like hot gel. They feel slimy. They feel like coagulated blood. Blood that has been exposed to oxygen for too long. It's disgusting."

"That is disgusting." I winced.

"Yeah! You're telling me! They sank their teeth into me and sucked my blood for months!" He laughed.

"So, you are saying that vampires are real and they are roaming the streets of Orange County right now?"

"No. I'll explain. There are two powerful races here on Earth. One race is us. We are the Day Walkers. Human beings if you will. The other race--the Night Walkers--is known as the Jinn Race."

"The Jinn Race?" I was very confused.

"Yes--" He said, "--The Jinn Race."

"What is the Jinn Race?"

"Well, it is said that we are God's children here on Earth. What most people don't realize is that it only makes sense that if God has children that Satan has children as well."

"So, you're saying the creatures that were sucking on your blood in the middle of the night were Satan's children?"

"Yes, I believe so. Satan is one sneaky bastard. He appeals to a woman in the form she finds most attractive. He manipulates them and plants his seed in as many of women as possible. He can read your mind and your thoughts. He knows your desires. He knows what turns you on. He knows what you like."

"That makes a lot of sense."

"Yes. Satan is a complete sex addict. Fucks all day, every day! That filthy slimeball. He will do whatever it takes to get into a fertile womb."

"Very interesting."

"Yes, so because Satan is the King of Fornication, naturally, he has a lot of children."

"Maybe since you have the untainted, virgin blood that's why they wanted to suck on you, but that's *also* the reason why they couldn't change you over to their Satanic sex addict Army."

"Yes, I really don't know how else to explain it." He sipped on his Crown Royal.

"What do you think about all of this?" I asked the blonde woman.

"I think... that he's a very, very nice guy." She smiled nervously.

High School Reunion

"Darren! How are you doing?! Wow. I haven't seen you in ages!" I said in a fake tone of voice.

"I've been better--" He spoke quietly. His eyes were dead.

His face was sucked in. His teeth were chipped and brown.

He smelled like piss.

"What's going on with you?" I pretended to be sensitive about his poor life decisions but it was difficult.

"I've just been waiting for a bed to open up in this Christian Center in L.A." He was being extremely vague about admitting that he was going to a rehab facility.

"So you're still struggling with heroin?" I asked him.

He looked irritated.

"We're getting older now Darren. Our bodies, well, your body isn't going to bounce back from using drugs like when we were kids." I touched his shoulder.

"It's been a really rough year for me. My sister died and I don't know what to do with myself."

"Oh no...How did your sister die?" I asked.

"A heroin overdose." He admitted.

"You're coping with the loss of your sister who overdosed on heroine by using heroin?"

"You have no idea what it's like trying to kick this shit! You get sick for weeks at a time. You're never happy. All you think about is getting high." His voice trailed off.

I rounded the corner to drop off three Long Island Ice Teas and the girls sitting at the table I had known for over a decade.

"Sara! Jessica! Martha! It's so good to see you ladies! What's going on!?" The three girls had gained a minimum of twenty-five pounds apiece. They were bloated and red. It was obvious they drank a lot.

"Just raising my two little boys! They really wear me out! It's like every day they get more energetic. I don't even know how it's possible!" Sara went on, "Timmy is just over 25 months and Alexander is almost 13 months."

"You know you can just say that they're basically a little over 2 and 1 right?"

"What?" Sara asked. Her mouth was filled with bread.

"Oh nothing," I replied, "how about you, Jessica? What's going on in your life?"

Jessica's thighs were so large I could see the seams in her pants about to rip.

"About the same," she said, "my daughter Michelle is already 6 years old. Where does the time go?" She smiled.

"You know, I always thought that you and John were the cutest couple in the world!" I told her, "What a perfect example of high school sweethearts that managed to stay together and be happy!"

Her smile turned upside down.

"John and I divorced two years ago."

"What about you Martha? Motherhood looks good on you! How old is your son or daughter now?"

"I don't have any kids..." Martha replied.

"Well, it was great catching up with you ladies!"

I ran outside and heard an idiomatic voice behind me.

"WHAT DOES IT TAKE TO GET A DRINK AROUND HERE?!"

His deep forehead wrinkles led up to a bald, hairless scalp. I stared at his shiny, red face until he spoke again. He raised his eyebrows and smiled at me. It made the wrinkles even more cavernous.

"Oh, it's you! You fixed your teeth! Wow. You look great. I thought you moved up to Washington a while back!" He inquired.

"What do you want to drink, Shane?"

"A large Coors Light would be awesome. So, what have you been up to? You should let me take you out sometime."

"I'll be right back with your drink."

I disappeared into the sea of drunks before he could say anything else. Shane was the type of guy who never had to work hard for anything because he had wealthy parents. Girls were all over him because of the money so he never formed any genuine long lasting relationships.

"Here's your Coors Light." I handed him the large beer.

"Seriously, time has been good to you! You gotta let me get your number! I'll take you out to a nice sushi dinner and we'll see where things go from there." He was a terrible salesman.

"Your total is $9 dollars. Would you like me to start a tab for you?"

"I'll pay cash. So how long have you been back in town for?"

He handed me a $20 dollar bill.

"Too long." I answered back.

"Keep the change. Money means nothing to me. You can have it. So how about you give me your number since I left you such a good tip?"

His ego was a front for the desperate insecurity lurking underneath the surface. I could smell it from a mile away like a shit filled litter box.

"Money doesn't buy love. You should know that by now." I walked away and he began to shout at me.

"Are you serious? You're fucking ugly anyway! I can have any chick I want you bitch!" He pointed to himself.

"Thanks for the tip!" I waved goodbye. I saw another friend of mine sitting by himself at the bar.

"Gavin? What's the matter?" I asked.

He slowly turned his head to look at me.

"Why can't my life just be simple? I keep asking myself what I did to deserve all of this."

"What do you mean?"

"I ended things with my wife just after she gave birth to our second child. I'll make a long story very short. It was already really hard for me to come to terms with the fact that she was a stripper."

"I see."

"I am not saying that strippers are bad people. I know some of them have really big hearts, as well as tits."

"Tell me the rest of the story."

"One of her coworkers came to me in confidence and told me that she was fucking guys in the champagne room and sleeping with a lot of men on the side for money."

"Holy shit!"

"A couple months after we started the divorce process I found out that she was dating a Marine she met at the club the whole time we were together. She moved the kids in with him almost immediately. She told me that they were getting married. He was getting stationed in Texas and that she was taking the kids and going with him."

"Jesus Christ!"

"I didn't have the money for a lawyer. The courts favored her even though she's a prostitute. Before I knew it, I was spending my last week with the kids."

"That's terrible."

"Oh, this isn't even the worst part." He took a shot.

"What?"

"So after a couple months I started dating this girl I had a major crush on in high school. She had a little boy and the kid's father had bailed out on her so I think things got serious really quickly because we bonded over that. Even though I was really skeptical about everything..."

"Why were you so skeptical?"

"Well--Because she was a stripper."

"I see..."

"I know. I know. I know. I love crazy girls what can I say. Believe me, I've beaten myself up enough already."

"Okay, so what happened next?"

"Things were going really well actually. We all moved into an apartment together and I felt like I had a family again. I missed my own family so much I wanted that feeling back at any cost. She seemed like she wanted the same thing as much as I did so I decided to propose to her."

"Stop. You did not."

"I KNOW! I KNOW! I'm an idiot!" He flung his head into his hands.

"Continue the story." I said.

"I asked her to marry me and of course she said yes. A week later I had a custom engagement ring made for her and planned to give it to her over a romantic dinner. The day before our dinner plans I had worked a fourteen-hour day in construction. I was so exhausted when I got home I went upstairs and immediately went to sleep. At some point during the night I woke up and heard strange noises coming from downstairs."

"Oh no." I covered my mouth.

"Something in my gut told me to get up and check it out. I walked out the bedroom door to see what was going on downstairs and that's when I heard her moaning--"

"No!"

"--I ran downstairs and there she was! Completely naked getting fucked by some random dude on the couch I had just bought!"

"No!"

"I started beating the hell out of him. He was begging me to stop. There was blood all over the place. I blacked out from all the rage and when I came to I was strangling him. The blood vessels in his eyes had popped. She was screaming naked in the background saying, 'I'm calling the police! You're going to kill him! I'm calling the police!' It was at this point reality hit me and I let go of his throat. I'm on probation and so I grabbed what clothes I could find and ran out of the house as quickly as I could."

"What happened to the guy?"

"Hell if I know. His face is burned into my memory though. He better pray that he doesn't run into me anywhere. But hold on, this still isn't even the worst part."

"There's no way this can get worse."

"Girl I told you. My life sucks. After all of this happened I told her that we were over. I didn't talk to her for about a month. That's when she called me and told me that she was pregnant with my third child."

"WHAT!"

"I know. I know."

"You need a vasectomy. Please tell me she got an abortion."

"Not exactly." He replied.

"What do you mean, not exactly? It's either yes or no. There's no such thing as a not exactly abortion."

"She hung it over my head for a couple weeks and begged me to take her back. I'm an idiot so I did."

"But I thought you weren't together anymore."

"We're not. She cheated on me again, while she was 3 months pregnant."

"I can't feel bad for you anymore." I told him.

"From what I hear she's currently trying to party the baby out. That's what her friends have told me."

"Party the baby out? What does that even mean?"

"I guess she's drinking, smoking, and doing a lot of cocaine and pills in hopes of miscarrying."

"She's a stripper! Doesn't she make enough money to go and get a good ol' fashioned planned parenthood abortion like all the other young women in southern California?"

"I think she's just in denial or something."

"You need a vasectomy, Gavin"

"I know--Believe me, I know." He looked disappointed.

I gave him a long, heartfelt hug.

I was enveloped once more

        by the vast ocean of sloshed chum

         People were flirting

           People were crying

             People were laughing

They were all trying to prove

     to one another

        that they had made it

         even though

          they hadn't

They were all mindlessly swaying back and forth

     eating each other's shit

        in this giant fish tank

          thinking they were too sly

           to ever get caught

            on The Hook

I wondered if they would ever wake up
or if this was it for them.

Easter Sunday

She was all alone, sobbing uncontrollably in the middle of the bar. There were several empty shot glasses strewn around her. Tears ran down her face as she desperately tried to regain what was left of her sanity.

I asked if she was okay.

She lit a cigarette.

"I'm nothing but a host at some stupid restaurant for old people!"

I wrapped my arms around her so tightly that the air came out of her lungs and she spit into my ear. I embraced her with everything I had.

"EVERYTHING WILL BE ALRIGHT." I told her as I wiped away her tears.

I knew her torment. I was a host for years. I looked into her eyes. One of her eyes looked back into mine.

Her other eye was floating to the left.

She took a shot of tequila and lit another cigarette.

"Seriously, everyone that comes into this place is over the age of 65. They're rude, demanding, and they stink like death!" She looked into the distance.

I gasped. I threw my hands up in the air and fell down to my knees. My stomach turned over. I felt sick.

I thought about all of the 5-10% tips and felt like I was going to throw up.

"TODAY WAS THE WORST DAY OF MY ENTIRE LIFE! HAVE YOU EVER WORKED AN EASTER SUNDAY AT RESTAURANT FOR SENIOR CITIZENS? IT IS HELL ON EARTH! I WORKED FOR 15 HOURS TODAY WITH NO BREAK!" She started to hiccup.

She leaned in and began to speak softly.

"I couldn't help it. I had to do what I had to do."

"What did you do?" I asked.

"I had to have my revenge." She went on. "At this point everyone had completely lost their cool. Orders were coming out totally wrong, time after time. Some of the food tickets were just... lost forever. The cooks were furiously swinging pots and pans around in the kitchen like Roman Gladiators. Bacon and eggs were flying all over the place. One of the kitchen staff chucked his spatula, quit his job right there on the spot, kicked open the back door and stomped out never to be seen again. They were sweating so hard they could barely see the grills. It was smoldering hot and dangerous back there."

"Oh god!" I started to shake.

I was having PTSD flashbacks of all the past Easter Sundays I had bravely fought myself.

She lit her third cigarette and continued her story.

"The servers were all running as fast as they could to prepare the side salads and soups--but they just weren't humanly fast enough to complete all of the tasks at hand. Every section and every table was full to the brim. It was a fucking battlezone. Everyone needed drink refills. There were no napkins to be found anywhere. The coffee wasn't hot. The Quiche was cold. The empty dishes from people's tables kept piling up and piling up. I walked into the cooler and chugged enough champagne to put down my aunt Samantha and then I hit myself in the head with the bottle repeatedly until I nearly knocked myself out. Walk in parties of twenty kept rolling in and rolling in like tidal waves. I knew I was going to die--At this point I was ten hours into my shift. I was covered in maple syrup from head to toe. The servers couldn't handle the high-volume intensity so I had to really jump in there and help. As I was running food to one of their tables, I put this man's plate down and he slammed his fist down onto the table so hard that it frightened me and I jumped. He said to me, 'I SAID I WANTED A FUCKING SIDE OF MAYONNAISE! AND GET ME A FUCKING WATER TOO WHILE YOU'RE AT IT! IS EVERYONE HERE STUPID OR SOMETHING?' That was it for me. My intelligence was being judged by a side of mayonnaise that never made it to a table? I went to the bathroom and started to cry. I wasn't crying because I was sad. I was crying because I was angry. It's such a cruel world we live in. Didn't that man see what was going on around him? Didn't he see that there were over 400 people all trying to eat at the same exact time? I couldn't be strong any longer. That's why I had to do what I had to do."

"So did you quit right there and walk out!?" I asked her.

"Absolutely not. I am no quitter. My mother always told me never give up. I was still crying pretty intensely in the bathroom but I stuck my finger into my asshole as far as I could and swirled it around." She made a swirling motion with her finger. "I left the bathroom and got the water and the side of mayonnaise ready for that crotchety old fuck and then I stuck my shitty finger into his water and stirred it around until I felt happy again. Eat my shit you piece of shit!" She screamed and flailed her arms around in the air.

"Well, it's all over now." I sighed as I reached across the table to remove the empty shot glasses.

She lit her fourth cigarette.

She inhaled hard and long.

She exhaled slowly and leaned backwards.

"It's never over."

Please Go Home By Killarney Tender

'Would you like another one?' I say in a slightly high pitched voice.

Somebody once told me you can tell when a person is lying when their voice becomes high pitched. Isn't that the truth?

I am an imposter of light.

I don't even make eye contact with them.

It's like I'm not talking to real people.

Just skeletons of people.

They don't hear my voice anyway.

They just hear their own.

If they can even hear their own anymore.

It's a soft whisper.

A small nagging if you will.

Just one more. Nobody is going to judge you.

What's the harm? You don't have a problem.

I want to tell them to get the hell out of here.

I want to tell them to go home from work early and play catch with their son.

I want to tell them to call their wife and tell her they love her and surprise her with a date tonight.

I want them to go away.

I want to hand them secret notes for the next local meeting, with their tip folded up inside.

I want to scream. No, you cannot have another.

Darkness is the absence of light. I can no longer live in this darkness.

A Middle-Aged Love Affair

"Good afternoon I will be your server today, may I start a beverage for you?" My introduction was weak.

The abnormally hot, middle-aged blonde woman sitting at the table ignores me. She pulls her long dress up above her hip and exposes a new tattoo to her date.

"I got this yesterday--" She says. "--hurt like a bitch."

"Wow that is so sexy. Do you have any other ones?" He asks.

"Yes, my daughter and I got matching ones on our feet."

She puts her foot onto his crotch and explains the meaning behind the Infinity symbol with pink flowers.

"Yea--I have a lot of tattoos myself--mostly from when I was in the Navy." He tells her.

"Oh yeah, like what?" She leans into him.

"Good afternoon I will be your server today, may I start a beverage for you?" I try again.

"I need the most expensive Chardonnay you've got--I'm allergic to sulfates." She winks at me.

"I'd like an O'Douls in a cold pint glass with a salted rim." He requests.

"No problem." I reply unenthusiastically.

"And a couple of limes too!" The man hollers.

I bring the drinks back.

The man licks his lips and stares at my tits.

His date asks me where the restroom is.

Just as she is out of ear's length the Gentleman tells me what an exquisite ass I have and that if he were my age he would rip it to pieces.

"Were you thinking of ordering any food today, sir?" I change the subject.

"Uhhhh...I don't know. Do you have any super cheap happy hour food?" He scratches his balls.

"Happy hour is over, sir." I break the news to him.

The man gets up to use the restroom and just as he is out of ear's length the woman returns and looks me dead in the eye--

"DO NOT EVER MEET ANYONE FROM MATCH.COM."

She chugs the wine.

"THIS GUY IS A LIAR! HIS PROFILE SAID HE HAD NO KIDS! HE'S FIFTY-TWO AND JUST TOLD ME RIGHT NOW THAT HE'S GOT A THREE-YEAR-OLD! I'VE RAISED SIX KIDS! I'M DONE RAISING KIDS! I WANT TO STAY UP LATE, DRINK WINE AND DO WHAT I PLEASE! HE'S SO ARGUMENTATIVE! YOU KNOW HOW SOME GUYS JUST WANT TO ARGUE ABOUT EVERYTHING?! HE KEEPS TRYING TO GET SOME NONEXISTENT POINT ACROSS EVERY TIME HE OPENS HIS MOUTH! I THINK HE'S HIGH! WHEN HE CAME TO PICK ME UP HE DIDN'T EVEN COME TO MY FRONT DOOR! HE CALLED ME AND SAID HE WAS OUTSIDE. WHEN I CAME OUT HE DIDN'T EVEN HUG ME! HE DIDN'T SHAKE MY HAND; HE WAVED AT ME AND GOT BACK INTO HIS CAR. HE DIDN'T OPEN MY DOOR FOR ME. I STOOD OUTSIDE OF HIS CAR AND STARED AT HIM LIKE HE WAS FUCKING RETARDED. FINALLY, HE ASKED ME IF I WANTED HIM TO OPEN MY DOOR FOR ME. I WAS LIKE UMMMMM YA?????? THAT'S HOW I RAISED MY SONS! SCREW THIS GUY. WHEN HE COMES BACK, I'M GOING TO TELL HIM I'M NOT INTO THIS. COULD YOU DO ME A FAVOR AND CALL A TAXI? THERE'S A REASON WHY THIS DOUCHE ENDED UP ON MATCH.COM."

The man comes walking back to the table with a large, stupid, confident smile on his face.

"Did you miss me while I was gone bebe?" He asks.

He thought he was so awesome.

"This isn't going to work out AT ALL!" She blurts out.

"Why not bebe? I thought we were havin' a good time?"

His facial expression shifts to confusion.

"No, sweetie. You're having a good time. I find you abrasive and argumentative."

"Whoa. Whoa. Whoa. I am not argumentative at all, nor am I abrasive." He defends himself.

"There you go again! Also, you didn't mention anything about having a three-year-old son! Your profile says you have ZERO KIDS! That was part of the reason why I decided to come on this date tonight!"

"Well, YOUR profile isn't exactly 100% accurate either, *sweetie*." He folds his arms.

"OH YEAH, LIKE WHAT? I'M NOT EVEN WEARING MAKE UP IN MOST OF MY PICTURES!" She starts to squawk.

"I don't know. Stuff. No one's profile is 100% accurate." His voice trails off.

"MINE IS! I AM DONE HERE! HAVE A NICE DAY! YOU PATHETIC LOSER, JACKOFF!" She grabs her purse and stands up.

"You're insane." He slams the remainder of his disgusting salty O'Douls.

"Pay for my Chardonnay and your tab too, Dick!" She demands.

"Hey toots, get over here. Cash me out right now." He snaps his fingers at me.

After one fatal swipe of the MasterCard he had been completely emasculated by the hot, empowered, 48-year-old blonde off Match.com.

Her long dress sparkled in the sun light and every man lounging at the patio bar turned their heads as she exited the vicinity.

She didn't need him anyway.

I could hear baby birds chirping enthusiastically in their nests.

Mama will be home soon little ones.

The squirrels were chasing each other up and down the trees.

Kids were drinking soda pop.

Old people were snoring.

The beloved regulars sat in their usual designated spots.

They smiled with me as we watched the performance come to a close.

Cigarette smoke plumed into the sky like Hiroshima.

The stage was theirs.

They played it well.

Just Move More Quickly

Dark red lipstick is my warpaint

I go to serve the masses but the masses serve me

Lost and confused I forgot the vodka soda

The death glare burns a hole into my back until I bring the liquor STAT

Here you go sir--won't happen again

'Puta' is the word I hear--when I ask for some extra French fries in the kitchen

The cooks put the bleu cheese on the meat and I admit defeat

The late-night snack hunger pain has come to play its game-- Once again

Does it ever end?

I wear buffalo sauce on my face like a clown

Would you like another Jaeger Bomb?

As the blessed time of last call approaches I soar through the patio like a bat out of hell

No more shots of Patron to the dome

No more tequila--I'm a believer in a good night's rest and pockets full of cash

Will I make it to last call?

An Expensive Hotel Steak

"Tell me a nasty story from when you worked at the kitchen in the hotel." I asked him.

He lit a cigarette.

He was a handsome Irishman with a heavy accent.

He stood 6'4 with salt and peppered hair. All of the ladies loved him. Sometimes he and I would be conversing and I would have absolutely no idea what he was talking about. He would begin to laugh out loud so I would laugh too, even though I had no idea what was going on.

"Well," He went on, "The server comes back to the kitchen and tells us he's gotta crankyass business man out there who wants his steak very well done. That didn't seem too hard. It was an upscale hotel. This is a $40 steak we're talking about here. Only windowlickers and Persians order their steaks well done. Anyway, we cook the steak very well done as instructed. The server came back to the kitchen about five minutes later and looked quite irritated. He said it's not well done enough. His eye was twitchin' hard I could tell he was stressed. We all looked back and forth at each other. Seriously? We put the steak back on the grill and cooked it for another fifteen minutes. It was very, very well done this time. We sent the steak off with the server. The server came back in less than a minute, lookin' like he was about to kill himself.

'CHAR THIS FUCKING THING UNTIL THERES NOTHING LEFT! BURN IT TO A CRISP!' He said.

So we burned the damn steak for another 20 minutes until it was a black, tough, crusty piece of leather. The server politely thanked us. He turned away and pulled his cock out of his uniform and slapped it on the steak about ten times. Then he took out his nuts and ran them across the meat. This was a nice guy we're talking about here. I had never seen him do anythin' like that before. I get it though; some people really get under your skin. Anyway, he put his cock and balls back in his pants and straightened out his work clothes. He went to the sink and washed his hands before he ran the food, I mean, that was gracious of him and all, but I don't know what the point was after all the cock slappin'! The server delivered the steak and told us the gentleman said it was perfect this time around." He laughed hard.

It was August and the air was salty and hot.

All the single girls were drinking vodka sodas.

They all wore different colored high waisted shorts.

Was I the only one out there in the world who passionately hated high waisted shorts?

I felt so alone.

I had felt alone most of my life--

but that didn't stop me.

A Dinner for Lona

"EXCUSE ME!" I hear the impatient voice of an old female vulture as she grabs onto my shirt.

Sitting before me is a man and woman.

The man is aggressively scarfing down pork ribs and coleslaw.

He is wearing tattered overalls with a holed Grateful Dead shirt underneath.

He is balding but that doesn't stop him from keeping his hair long.

The woman's enormous tits are hanging down to her belly button and they are swaying from side to side.

She is wearing a thigh length tie dye t-shirt as a dress with pink bed slippers.

They both look like they stepped out of time capsule from 1969.

"We wanted to know about the birthday dinner deal! We read the sign on the wall. Could you tell us more about it?" She inquires.

They had an impressive amount of food particles stuck in their rotten brown teeth.

"Well, you come in the night of your birthday and we will honor a free entree!"

I give them jazz hands and smile.

There was a blackboard hanging on the wall.

When there was an upcoming birthday we would scribble people's names on it to make them feel special and appreciated.

"May I put the name Lona up on the birthday board and we'll come back next week for steak and shrimp?" The woman asks me.

"Sure! Is your name Lona? I've always liked that name." I say to her.

"No, my dead mother's name is Lona. She's been gone for about seven years now, but I just wanted to come and eat a free meal in honor of her. She was a real hard bitch, you know? Still...she was my mother nonetheless. The only things I think she ever really, *truly* loved were her damn chickens!"

She got up and started to write 'Mama Lona' on the board.

They began to laugh.

They paid the bill and I watched them waddle out the front door like fat, stupid penguins.

In honor of Mama Lona--

I erased her name from the blackboard.

Puppy Tongue Part II of II

I saw a small man standing in the entryway.

He was facing to the left and I could not see his face.

"Have you been helped today, Sir?" I asked.

He slowly turned his head in my direction.

The roughened, cadmium red skin around his eye sockets wrinkled up as the crowing grin spread across his face.

He was holding a black notebook under his arm.

"I was hoping you'd be here tonight. I have returned with a gift for you my Queen, just as promised."

He glided across the floor in my direction.

"Inside of this envelope are two different stories. One of the stories is about your first love. The other story is called, 'Birds of a Feather'. It's about me bringing a woman to orgasm with only a feather. Now, these are a gift young lady. Do not steal my stories and use them as your own! I've had bad experiences with people taking credit for my stories. I'd be a millionaire three times over had I known more about copyright laws!"

He handed me the envelope and before I could say anything he embraced me. He reeked of salt water and bird poop.

"I can smell your B.O. and I love it!" He said to me.

He pulled me in closer and licked my neck.

I backhanded him hard like a disobedient stepchild.

He looked a little stunned.

I could tell he had already been drinking quite a bit.

"I'm sorry baby; it has been a horrible day. Do you have a moment for an old, stupid piece of shit like myself?" He pleaded.

He was vulnerable.

I got him a Whiskey.

"I only fall in love with demonic married women. It's been the curse that has ruined my life. My first love wouldn't leave her husband even though he almost beat her to death." He started to cry.

"I told her I would kill him, I couldn't handle watching her suffer anymore. She was an angel. Bat shit crazy, but an angel. I didn't deserve her, but for some reason she chose me. That was enough reason for me to end his life."

He cried harder.

"She called me sobbing uncontrollably and told me to come over. I sped quickly to her house and when I got there she had hung herself with a jump rope in her bedroom. Pills were strewn across the floor. "

He started to work his hand up my thigh. I grabbed his hand and twisted it so hard he fell off his chair.

"Are you really making a move on me in the midst of crying about your first love's suicide, Puppy Tongue?!"

"I'm bad baby, I know! I can't help myself. I am but a man! At least I am an honest man."

He picked himself up off the ground.

Two beautiful girls came to Puppy Tongues aid.

"That was quite the tumble you took sir, are you okay?"

One of the girls asked.

"I could make you cum with just a feather." He replied to the girl.

"Excuse me?!" Her friend butted in.

"I didn't stutter. You heard me! I said I could make you cum with just a feather!"

"Who do you think you are talking to a woman like that? Do you know who she--"

"--Shut the fuck up! I can tell just by looking into your scared, passionless eyes! You have never experienced a deep, bone chilling orgasm that makes you realize there is a purpose for you here on this Earth! The kind of full bodied, trancelike orgasm that leaves you blind, deaf, and dumb as fuck! The kind of orgasm that confirms that there's something more out there. Something far beyond us! Far beyond this stupid bar and your twenty-one-year-old tits! Have you ever experienced anything like that before?! Have you ever felt that way in all your life?"

"You're fucking weird!" One of the girls yelled at him.

"TELL ME I'M WRONG!" Puppy Tongue yelled louder.

"That's all you'll ever wrap your mind around is eating your own shit. You're just another copy of a cheap, unoriginal copy. I can smell your fear. You're afraid to wake up and taste the foul morning breath of your lover! You're weak!"

One of the girls threw her drink in his face.

"Once all of your lovers are dead you'll wish you would have appreciated that putrid taste of their mouth a little more!" He raised his Whiskey.

"Here's to *real* love! You fake cunts!" He slammed the shot.

"You really know how to make an impression on people." I said to him.

"After my first love committed suicide I swore I would never allow myself to feel that way about another human being again." He continued his story without skipping a beat. "I spent most of that time alone, traveling by myself. After a while I came back out of my shell and started to sleep with all sorts of women. I started to accept the touch of a human being again. Twenty-five years later on the anniversary of my first love's suicide, I decided to call back my fondest memories of her by getting blacked out drunk on my boat in the harbor. As I sat there, horrified and alone, a gorgeous, leggy redhead approached me. I was seeing triple, but I swear to whatever God there is that the sky opened up around her. She smiled the most brilliantly wild smile I had ever witnessed. She climbed onto my boat without saying a word. She wiped the tears away from my eyes and grabbed the bottle of Whiskey out of my hand. She took five enormous gulps of liquor without flinching and when she finally came up for air she kissed me so hard we almost fell over. She pulled me underneath the cabin and tore my clothes off. She rode me like no woman had ever ridden me before. She rode me like she resented me forever. She rode me like she worshiped Christ. She slapped me across the face as she came." He was still in awe of the memory.

"And none of this was a red flag to you?" I asked.

"I knew she was going to be trouble but I didn't care about anything anymore. I wanted to feel something real. I knew she wasn't faking it. She knew about her magic powers. I could feel that her misery went so much deeper than mine. She told me that she was married. Her husband beat her senseless but she had a very rare form of blood cancer that wasn't going away no matter how aggressive the treatment was. She couldn't save the money or make a plan to leave him because she was so sick. I stayed with her even through the worst parts of the cancer. She wouldn't leave her husband and I couldn't watch her die so I tried to end things with her and she won't let me. Now she's threatening to kill herself too. She knows my first love killed herself and that I'm weak to those threats. I'll do anything she tells me to, I love her."

He dropped his cigar on the ground and a tall brunette picked it up for him.

"Here you go sir, are you okay? You look like you're having a rough night." She asked him.

"Mind your own business, bitch. What do you know about love? What do you know about pain?" He mumbled.

"No, *Bro*! *You* mind *your* own business!" The brunette's boyfriend chimed in.

Puppy Tongue pulled a switchblade out of his pocket.

"How about I make it my business and fucking kill you?!"

He screamed as tears ran down his cheeks.

In an instant the boyfriend picked Puppy Tongue up off of the ground and slammed him down hard onto the floor.

He dropped the knife on impact and it slid under one of the tables.

His head bounced against the cement so forcefully it sounded like a gunshot went off.

He somehow got up and collected himself.

He cried out:
> "YOU HAVE NO IDEA--
>
> WHAT TRUE LOVE MEANS!"

He spit a mouthful blood onto the ground.

He ran out the back door to his van and drove out of the parking lot so fast that his tires squealed.

I went home that night and kept thinking about the sound that his skull made as it cracked against the floor.

That noise sounded over and over in my ears.

Bone and rock colliding.

I stared at the envelope that Puppy Tongue had given me.

I found the bravery somewhere within myself to open it.

Inside the envelope, the stories were wrapped in tin foil.

Inside of the tin foil, the pages were folded shut.

As I unfolded them I saw that the paper was carefully burned along the edges and soaked with a strong, floral fragrance.

I started to sweat.

I saw the title of my story,

which read,

'Fourteen'.

How would my most intimate experience

be interpreted in words

by someone who never knew me at all?

What did I really know about love anyway?

Through the Looking Glass

The three men were in their mid-50's.

They were handsome and clean-cut.

They looked like they were on a team together.

Their hair was the same peppered grey color, and they were all wearing expensive, dark blue-holed jeans paired with slim fit black t-shirts.

One of them was really tall, one of them was really small, and the other man was average height.

"I'm Tall Tim."

"I'm Small Steve."

"And last but not least I'm Medium Mike." They all laughed in unison.

Medium Mike was showing Small Steve a picture of something on his phone. They were laughing very loud so I asked what they were looking at.

Medium Mike jerked the phone away very quickly and said, "I can't show you, you'll think we're horrible people."

"Is it a naked picture of someone?" I asked.

"No not this time. I have some naked pictures of my son's girlfriend on here though. It's pretty good stuff."

"You're lying."

"My son and I are very close; do you want to see?"

"No. I asked what you were looking at--PRESENTLY."

"Okay fine. I'll show you, but I promise that we are good guys."

He reluctantly handed over his phone.

I took a glance at the screen and was immensely disappointed in the lack of originality.

I handed him back the phone.

"Let me remind you that I work at a bar, gentlemen. That's all you've got? I see this shit every night. Now come on! Really! I dare you. Put in some effort and *really* try to disturb me. Now, would you like another round of drinks to make this conversation more interesting or what?!"

They nodded their heads. I made three more cocktails.

"We don't have a picture to show, but we have a story for you. This will definitely disturb you." Small Steve said with confidence.

"I met this gorgeous older woman in Laguna Beach." Medium Mike went on. "We sat up at the bar and talked for a while. She was single and seemed pretty smart. She said that she owned a nice big house up on the hill with an ocean view. I bought her some drinks and after a while we started to make out. I offered her some cocaine and she said that we could go back to her house to party and drink more. When we got to her house, we did a ton of blow and things started to get weird."

Small Steve and Tall Tim started to laugh really hard.

"This story never gets old!" Their eyes began to water.

"What happened next?" I asked.

"Well, she told me that she wanted me to lie under the glass table in the living room while she took a shit on top of it."

"She wanted to shit on you?"

"No. She wanted to shit *on top of the table* while I lay *underneath it*." He corrected me.

"Did you let her do it?"

"Well, you know. When in Rome, isn't that what they say?" He shrugged his shoulders.

"You're telling me that you let a random woman from the bar take you back to her house and crap on you?"

"She was hot! It's not like she crapped *on me*! She crapped *on the table*!" He kept pointing out.

"So then what happened?"

"Well, then we fucked."

"You still had sex with her after she shit on the table?"

"Of course. I was not going to get almost shit on and not get anything in return." His logic was sound.

"I wonder how many men have laid under that table." I pondered.

"Oh man, I don't wanna know." Medium Mike sighed.

"At which point did she clean it?"

"Hell, I don't know. We went into the bedroom to have sex and I just never went back into the living room. I didn't want to know what she was going to do with it. It's not my business." Medium Mike laughed hysterically.

"Her poor cleaning lady..." Tall Tim said.

"May we please have another round of drinks, young lady?" Small Steve politely asked.

"Of course, I'll be right back."

"Why do you have a strange look on your face?" My coworker asked me.

"You see those three men over there?" I gestured to the trio.

"Yes." He glanced to the right.

"One of them just told me a story about this hot, successful, older lady that took him back to her house in Laguna Beach and made him lay under her glass table while she took a shit on top of it."

"That is not a real story." He said.

"I don't think they're lying about this one." I admitted.

"Why would any good-looking woman secretly coerce men back to her house to shit on them? That doesn't make any sense." He argued.

"It makes perfect sense." I said.

"How does that make perfect sense?" My coworker questioned me.

"This woman doesn't need any man. She already has every-thing that she needs. She has money, good looks, owns her own home and lives in one of the best places in America. This guy is completely disposable. She doesn't have to rely his acceptance, so there's no need to be delicate or polite. She's independent. Most women put up with the negative personality attributes of men because they're insecure and want someone to support them. Some men look at women as nothing more than objects of sex. They go out weekend after weekend to bars and clubs with the goal to screw as many women as possible. I'm sure at some point in that woman's life, she was taken advantage of. Her way of getting back at the world and to feel sexually liberated is to crap on random men from the bar. Men are so horny and easily influenced that they'll let a random woman crap on them. It's perfect."

"That does make sense." He agreed.

I wondered who this woman was
where she grew up
and if her parents were still married

I wondered what business she ran
I wondered who cleaned the poop
off her living room table

I wondered how many men she had crapped on
How did all of this begin?
I wondered if she was happy
or if she just thought she was happy

The Indian Summer had enveloped us all
We were all ready for the crispness of fall--
but it just wasn't coming soon enough

The bars were still packed
the people all yearned for something
anything
to help them sleep better at night

White Light by Killarney Tender

I walk knee deep through a sea of tables and chairs.

Lost—

but not alone.

'What the fuck is taking so long?' They all wonder.

'You'd move this slowly too--' I say under my breath.

I am a cross country skier, an Olympian of sorts, moving carefully through mountains of ranch dressing.

I march boldly making a track wherever I go.

My feet are Chicken Tenders.

The glasses start to wobble on my tray and I slow my turn.

I know where this is heading--noises cease and the white light begins to brighten.

The end is coming.

Memories of trays lost in the past blossom in my mind like bean sprouts in a time lapse video.

The glasses begin to crash--one by one--eternity between pauses.

I imagine myself as a hot air balloon, free from the weight of the world.

I imagine myself as a dove--peaceful--serene--

Reality hits with a shatter

and I am nothing

but a boneless tender—

drowning in a sea of bleu cheese.

And I am looking for you--

The Most Ugly Girl I've Ever Seen

My cousin Chuck and my boyfriend Aj decided that we were going to have a drinking contest.

We sat around the fire polishing off bottles of cheap Whiskey. We threw the empty glasses at the hot embers.

We put gasoline in the fire.

We spat in the fire.

We peed on the fire.

We fed it so much wood the flames became extravagant and mesmerizing.

We gave it a name; its name was Grace.

We laughed until snot flew out of our noses.

We were sharing stories about our pasts.

We started sharing stories about our ex-lovers.

Aj started to talk about a girl that he once dated that had the voice of an angel. My cousin asked to see a photo of her so Aj found one. She was a pretty girl.

"I'd fuck her." Chuck said.

"Such a gentleman." I laughed.

"Don't be jealous." Chuck came back at me.

"She's cute, but she doesn't upset me. You can find twenty girls like that down at 6th Ave on a Friday at Jazzbones." I retorted.

"You're totally right." Aj admitted. "She bore me to death. I stopped talking to her. I felt bad, she got all clingy and I literally just quit answering her calls. I guess I'm kind of a dick. She had amazing tits though man, they sat so nicely."

"Do you have a picture of her tits?" Chuck slurred.

"No I wish." Aj looked over at me. "Don't worry babe, your tits are way nicer."

He grabbed my breast like he was honking a horn.

"She has really nice teeth." I said.

"Yes, she does. But who are we kidding? You have the worst teeth that I have ever seen!!" Aj started laughing hysterically. My cousin joined in.

"Excuse me?" I felt a sword through my heart.

"Dude! Seriously... How did they even get so bad? Did you do a lot of drugs or something? I just don't understand how they got like that." Aj kept going.

"I was just born this way." I whimpered "How could you say that to me?" Their laughter continued.

"This was nature that did this to me not my own decisions. I had no choice in the matter." I yelled.

"Are you sure?" Aj asked as he and Chuck rolled around on the ground laughing at me.

I started to get the flashbacks from middle school.

I could hear the 6th graders making fun of me--

DONKEY TEETH.

Back in the day boys would say:

"Maybe I'll date her in a couple of years when her teeth aren't so fucked up."

I had always had really crooked teeth.

My parents chose a terrible bargain orthodontist that left my mouth mangled and strange.

I was an average looking girl with a hick smile. It was the reoccurring joke since as far back as I could remember.

DONKEY TEETH.

I heard it ringing in my ears.

I got up from the fire pit and went inside to get my belongings. I got my purse and marched out the front door. I didn't know where I was going to go. It was Friday night at 1:03am. I had to leave. Anywhere was better than being stuck with that cruel, cocksucking Army douche. I made it across the front lawn and that's when Aj and Chuck came running out the front door to try and stop me.

Chuck got to me first. He was still laughing.

I was in the midst of ripping him to pieces like a wild racoon when he hugged me from the back so hard I thought I was going to barf. I managed to kick him in the balls and he let go.

I screamed like Xena warrior princess as I went for Aj.

DONKEY TEETH.

I swung my shoes above my head by their laces like a helicopter. I hurled the shoes at Aj's face and they hit him so hard he started drooling. I took off my sweat shirt and tried to wrap it around his neck to strangle him with it. As I was squealing like the fiercest of Banshees, he tackled me to the ground.

"You need to chill the fuck out!!" He screamed into my face as he held me against the dirt.

"How could you say that to someone you claim to love Aj?!" I begged him for an answer.

"Your teeth are terrible! Do you want me to lie to you? What do you want me to say? They're nice? They're not!" He yelled at me.

DONKEY TEETH.

I kicked him in the nuts and crawled out from under him. I got up and started to run. I was crying so hard I accidentally threw myself into a ditch.

I screamed like someone was trying to murder me.
I thrashed my body like I had been poisoned.
I looked like the exorcist down there.
I was throwing a serious drunken fit at the bottom of that ditch when I realized I was in the center of deep, apical, needlelike bushes.

There were thick sticker bushes in every direction around me for at least six feet. Most of my body was exposed from removing articles of clothing to assault my boyfriend. I looked down and I was bleeding, from everywhere. There were gashes, scratches, and puncture wounds on me from head to toe.

I just wanted to be in a normal relationship.
He had seemed so charismatic at first.
I thought I was smarter than this. I was wrong.

I started sobbing harder.
I did all of this to myself.

Colossal thorns were lodged deeply into every inch of my scathed body.

How was I going to get out of these bushes?

I was scared to do it, but I tried to move. I started yelping immediately. Any movement provoked a different spiked branch to stab into a separate limb on my body. The simultaneous physical and psychological pain was the most excruciating torture I had ever experienced in my life.

I had lost.
I started hyperventilating.

My adrenaline was kicking in.

Somehow, I managed to get off of my back.
My legs and arms were torn to shreds.
I crawled my way out of that thorn hell shrieking in a high falsetto.
The pain had sobered me up.
Aj and Chuck helped me out once I got to the top.
I couldn't stand up because there were so many thorns stuck in the bottom of my feet.

Chuck put me over his shoulder like a rag doll and took me inside the house to the bathroom.

The light was off and everything was dark.
He set me down on the side of the bathtub and left me alone.
I locked the door behind him.

I took my clothes off. I turned on the light and what I saw, terrified me. I had to be dreaming. There was no way that reflection belonged to me.

I was someone else.
Someone from another unfamiliar dimension.
The girl in the mirror was a facade.

There were gashes ripped in every direction across my face. They were across my eyelids and across my lips. It looked like I had taken a razor blade and done this myself. The cuts on my wrists and hands were so excessive it looked like I was a self-butchering teenager crying for help.

I was the most ugly girl I had ever seen.
I got into the hot shower and everything started to sting.

I sat there for an hour with a pair of tweezers trying to pull out all of the deep-rooted thorns that made that their home in my ass.

I thought about all of the decisions I had made leading up til this point.
Had it all been worth it?
No.
I vowed this was the last time I would ever remove thorns from my eyelids.

That night I never really fell asleep.
My injuries burned every time I moved.
I cried when I would envision how I looked in that mirror.
I wondered if when I woke up in the morning all the cuts would be gone.
I wondered if all of this had actually happened to someone else.

I awoke the next day to a bouquet of Roses.
Aj looked down at me with the flowers in his hand and started laughing at me again.

"I'm sorry! I can't help it! You look absolutely insane!" He didn't even attempt to contain himself.

I had work that night.
When I walked through the door all of my coworkers face's turned upside down.

For the next three months I waited to look remotely normal.

Customers couldn't help but stare at my razored lips and eyelids. It was as if I could hear their thoughts.

Poor girl.
Her parents are probably divorced.
She probably listens to that awful devil music.
Look at her.
She never stood a chance in the world.

No one was rude to me for that period of time.

Even if they were mad, they never really showed it.

They'd start to get agitated about something so insignificant
and I would stare intensely into their eyes
with my torn, fucked up face
and they'd look away.

It became liberating.

No one could hurt me anymore.

I disappeared into the airy background of the stirring chaos
that had consumed me and learned how to embrace the quiet
solitude.

And when I finally emerged from my cocoon--

     I sprouted wings

         that could take me anywhere I desired.

Sharkfaces

From the darkest depths of my nightmares
I am looking at the computer screen
and the buttons move from underneath my finger

Nothing inputs correctly
I don't have time for this

There's a graveyard of bones
tickling my toes
as I tread these waters

I'm submerged in the salty dangerzone
with Great White predators on my tail
They all want more shots
They chomp at my limbs
like they've been starving for years

The customers rip me with their insults as I try and swim away

I can hear you bitch
You think you can do this better than me?
I dare you to try

I hit my head on the table as I clear the dirty dishes
People stifle their laughter
But they're still looking down on me
There is no justice in the world

The Wallflower

"We were sitting near the dumpsters smoking a cigarette on our break the other day and this weird guy approached us and started asking us all these bizarre questions. Like, have you ever had any experiences with ghosts? Have you ever felt like we were all just inside of a large, elaborate science experiment? What do you think that aliens think about us in our current state? What do you think the color of your aura is? We felt so awkward but of course we were nice to him. Yesterday he showed up and watched me work for hours. It was so creepy. Now he showed back up again! He keeps coming up to me and asking if I have eleven minutes to watch a video on his phone about schizophrenia. He's freaking me out. He doesn't want to buy any drinks from me; he just wants to talk about schizophrenia." My coworker told me.

"Find a security guard and ask him to leave if he's bothering you."

"I don't want to be too mean to the guy, he probably really does have schizophrenia or something." She sympathized with him.

"Probably." I agreed.

"I mean, he's *actually* kind of hot. But he's just too weird, I couldn't do it. He'd end of being one of those, slit your throat in the middle of the night types, you know what I mean?" She said.

"I know what you mean. That's why we should get him out now before he makes a decision about which girl's head he's going to put on a stick." I said.

I looked inside and our newest manager, Jason, was off the clock and drinking excessively.

He rode his bike everywhere and always wore very bright colored clothing.

At this moment in time he was wearing a luminescent salmon pink shirt, very short red reflective shorts with black leggings underneath, and a lime green helmet.

It was Saturday night and there was a full band playing.
He walked over, grabbed the microphone and started singing
along.
His voice was so off tune and belligerent that they turned off
the sound to his mic.
He was up there wailing into the microphone with no sound
but he was too drunk to notice.
He was dramatic about his stage presence.
He kicked his legs and he banged his head passionately.
He was two inches away from falling into the drums.

I suddenly became overwhelmingly aware of how absurd this
world truly was.

He staggered over to a group of women and fell on top of their
table. It was at that point the lead security guard escorted
Jason to the bathroom to collect himself. The security then
came outside to ask how Jason intended on getting home and
to start making arrangements because he needed to go. Within
three minutes one of the bartenders ran outside with a
concerned look on his face and whispered something into
security's ear. The security guard urgently ran inside.

"WHAT HAPPENED?" I asked.
The bartender looked down and told me.
"Jason fucked up."
"COME ON WHAT HAPPENED?" I asked again.
"These men came to the bar and told me that there was a
highly intoxicated autistic guy with a helmet on in the bath-
room with his dick out pissing all over the walls."
"...What did you just say to me?" I needed a confirmation.
"Those guys don't know that Jason is a manager here. If
anyone finds out about this, he's done for. Numerous people
just saw him in the bathroom with his bright ass lime green
helmet on, dick out, pissing all over everything! It's a busy
Saturday night!! For Christ's sake!"

This was the person responsible for me.
This was the person they chose to represent us professionally.
The company I was working for was falling apart.

Every day they were calling me to come in early or stay late because so and so quit or so and so didn't show up.

Sometimes I wondered if my life would be easier if I was unreliable.

Anytime anything went wrong I was the first person they'd call to try and pick up the pieces, and most times, I said yes.

But recently I had been running out of gas.
The person who was supposed to resolve issues and create solutions was painting the walls and sinks of the men's bathroom with his peepee.
I thought about how much I really needed this job.

There was a female's voice behind me I could hear very loudly.

"I just went into the women's restroom and I saw the most disgusting thing I've ever experienced in my life. Some chick in there was wearing a fancy yellow ball gown and had the front of it pulled up above her head so that she couldn't see. She stuck her hand into her panties and flicked a white glob of something across the bathroom and it hit the mirror. I'm never coming back to this place." She tossed her cigarette butt onto the ground, got up and left.

I had been living very minimally in hopes of saving money to travel around the U.S. and do something different with my life for little while.

The everyday stresses were making me bitter.
I began to feel like a fungus.
I had lost my flame.
Nothing was beautiful anymore.
The loss of sanity wasn't worth the money.

Security led Jason outside.

Jason had a lighter in his hand.
He leaned up against the handicapped parking sign in front of
the building.
He put the lighter to his head as if it was a cellphone.
He talked into the lighter and flicked it on.
He started to burn his hair.
"HELLO?" He yelled into the lighter.

He would take the lighter away from his head and look at it in
a puzzled fashion with one eye closed, and then put it back up
to his ear again.

"ARE YOU COMING TO GET ME?" He asked the lighter.

No one was coming for him--
and no one was coming for me either.

At some point during the night while someone was cleaning
the piss off the walls, I realized--
We all have an unlimited amount of power at the tips of our
fingers.

We must make it for ourselves in this world even though every
force of nature works against us.

It seems that everyone has forgotten

that life is about so much more

than all of this

stupid shit.

Every passing scenario

is a test

that stains the sheets

of the beds

we make for ourselves.

Be true to yourself and everything else will melt away

like fat after a gastric bypass surgery.

My time was coming.

I could feel the strong pull of my greatest adventure

yearning to take me.

I wanted it now--but I would have to wait--

just a little while longer.

Le Cirque Maudit III of III

"I must be dreaming." I sighed.

"This is as real as real gets. I've been doing this for a very long time. 7,665 years to be exact." Mkhail got up out of his seat.

"You are not 7,665 years old. This is getting tiresome. I am ready to wake up now." I folded my arms.

"Follow me; I want to show you something."

We walked outside of the tent.

We were in the center of the most marvelous Circus I had ever witnessed.

The colours were so vivid it was as if everything was aglow.

Every light on every contraption was bright and luminous.

The air was filled with the smell of cotton candy and funnel cake.

"Okay, I'll play along Mkhail. So you're telling me that I could sign The Contract and be given unlimited power at the cost of my soul?"

"No, not unlimited power. Power within reason, and not at the cost of your soul. Don't be so dramatic." He laughed.

"Power within reason?" I asked.

"It means you will have an unlimited amount of performance strength. You will never exhaust. You will never get injured, even if you fall and break your leg it will regenerate immediately. You will not appear to age, which is why Sofia and Penny still look beautiful and young. You will never grow weak even if you do not practice or eat."

"How long is The Contract?" I inquired.

"1,000 years."

"These women committed to a 1,000 year long contract?!"

"Hey now! 1,000 years isn't that long considering The Big Man gets them out of their horrid situations and gives them a chance to make things right again. Not to mention he gives them an opportunity to live out their dreams performing to their fullest potentials in the best Circus in the whole wide world! Sofia doesn't have to be paralyzed anymore and Penny doesn't have to get beaten up and live with her sick, deformed baby. It works out great for everyone."

"I noticed that there are only women in this Circus."

"We keep the genders separate." He told me.

"Why?" I asked.

"People fall in love and things become too complicated."

"How so?"

"It's hard enough for two people to get along within one lifetime let alone an equivalent of about 100 human lifetimes. Could you possibly imagine the drama that takes place when you stick a group of 3 women and 3 men together for 1,000 years?" He posed.

"Actually no, that sounds horrible." He had a point.

"Plus we have enough problems with males who haven't signed The Contract falling in love with the girls."

"What do you mean by that?"

"The girls will always fall in love with a man somewhere at some point. The men are transfixed on the women because of their beauty and mysteriousness. Although the women have superhuman abilities, of course they still crave the touch of a man."

"Well yes, of course."

"If one of the girls falls in love, they permeate an intense, irresistible sexual Energy that draws the men towards them. These men will follow the Circus around from city to city, fighting for a single moment to approach the girls. The girls will find opportunities to run away with these men. It works for a while, but then he begins to age while she stays the same. It's a losing battle from the beginning. Plus, I always hunt them down and find them eventually."

"Can't you just wipe the memory of the girls from the men's mind? I thought you said that once you signed The Contract nobody would remember who the girls were and they would cease to exist in the world they once lived in?"

"Yes, they cease to exist in the world they *once* lived in. Unfortunately if a man is genuinely in love with one of the girls there is nothing we can do about that. Love trumps the power of the Big Man and myself. The only option at that point is to travel as far away from the men as possible so that we can wait patiently for them to die."

"That is so sad. Why not just let them be in love for a little while?" I asked.

"I tried that a long time ago and it never ended well. Everything got of hand. There was one girl, Diana. She fell in love 36 times in a period of 1,000 years with the same five men! That was the most despair I had ever witnessed from a single woman. It was like she was cursed. The amount of loss she experienced was so extensive. 2 years after barely recovering from the loss of her third love, she'd find her first love for the

4th time in another country! The situations were so endlessly bizarre. She used to cry so much. It drove me insane..."

"The men didn't remember her when they were meeting for the second, third and fourth time?" I asked.

"It is another part of The Contract. If you meet someone again in their next life, even if you want to, your mouth will not allow you to say anything that would reveal that truth."

"Why?"

"It messes with The Grand Scheme of Things."

"But love is an essential part of our existence." I stated.

"Yes, but that was totally unnatural. In a normal situation with an average lifespan nothing like that would have ever occurred. Therefore, we keep the genders separate. During my first contract, I fell in love with a woman so deeply I traveled to the ends of the world to try and be with her--I was kidding myself. One day I will get the opportunity to try it all again."

"How many women have you been in love with since this whole creepy career path started for you 7,665 years ago?" I asked him.

"Only one. That's why this job comes so easily for me. Most human beings, in their infinite amount of lives, will fall in love with the same seven people, life after life. That is why when people are deeply in love, they feel like they have known each other forever. It is because they have actually known one another for all of eternity."

"Without love, we are nothing." I muttered.

"Perhaps you are right."

"Why don't you be with her now?" I suggested.

"There is no point in pursuing her until this Contract is over."
He replied.

"Why?"

"My interactions with her have always directly resulted in her death. I tried a couple different times and it was the same outcome. There's a reason why I do this job. Tragedy follows me. Even when I wasn't working for The Big Man I was still a very, very unlucky person. It's easier to be alone. I had to stop myself from pursuing her when she would finally emerge into the world again. It's excruciating to watch someone die repeatedly knowing you're the only one to blame."

"Where is she now?" I inquired.

"She's dead right now."

"What do you mean she's dead *right now*?"

"What I mean by that is, she was once alive, right now she is dead, and in the future she will live again. She is taking a break right now. But her energy is everywhere; I can still feel her right now even as we speak."

"You said that one day she will be back?"

"We all come back. We live an infinite amount of lives, and those lives vastly differ from each other and mirror the other life's we are living elsewhere in an infinite amount of dimensions--forever and ever." He looked at me seriously.

"What the fuck are you talking about?"

"Is that so hard to believe?" He asked me.

"You're a car salesman and I can smell it." I pointed my finger in his face.

"I have never sold a car in my entire 7,665 years."

"Alright, sure. So then what is your story Mkhail? How did you become the Ring Leader of this Circus?"

"I am not the Ring Leader actually; I just work for The Big Man."

"Who is the The Big Man?"

"The Big Man is the one behind the scenes that is actually running the whole show."

"How did you start working for the Big Man?" I asked jokingly.

"After my first Contract was up I decided that I wanted to renew and sign another one. The benefits and rewards of the renewed Contract give me more abilities and also give me more freedoms as well." He responded.

"I guess I'm just a lifer." He laughed hard at his own joke.

"So, if you have all of this power, why weren't you able to locate Sofia more quickly? Why did it take you so long to find her?"

"The Contract is the same for me as well, although I have more power, it is still power within reason. I can sense when she is further away or closer to me, but I cannot pinpoint her specific location." He told me.

"That sucks for you!" I giggled.

"Well, luckily for me, the girls cannot sense if I am further away or closer to them so I have the advantage when they run away. It makes things fun and challenging!"

He smiled and rubbed his hands together.

"Nothing about this is reasonable." I sighed.

"You have been told forever that you are supposed to live reasonably when in fact life is the most unreasonable, unpredictable mechanism that drives this reality forward."

"You know, I have to admit. I am really impressed with myself considering you are a complete figment of my imagination. But I'll keep playing along. What does The Big Man get out of all this?" I asked.

"Energy." Mkhail replied.

"Energy?"

"Energy to keep this Grand Illusion going on forever and ever."

"Why would I ever agree to any of this?"

"Have you ever listened to an incredible musician, been in awe of an Olympic athlete or seen a famous artist's work and wondered, how is it possible for those people to be so talented?" He asked me.

"Of course." I admitted again.

"Let me tell you something darling. They all signed The Contract. They just have no memory of it now." He stated.

"Every exceptionally talented person signs The Contract? How could I ever believe that?"

"It's all about progression. What are you willing to sacrifice for greatness? That is what it comes down to. That's another perk to this Contract." He went on, " Once your Contract is up, you have two options: You can either renew or you can start back on Earth and be born on the year of your choice, in the place of your choice--with all of the talents you worked on for the last 1,000 of years. Your skills will stay intact for the rest of Eternity!"

"This is the part where I ask about the negatives, Mkhail."

"The negatives are that you have no memories of The Contract and you have no memories of any of the experiences and events within the 1,000 years. Another negative is that you cannot dictate the course of your next life so it could potentially, worst case scenario, become a completely wasted talent."

"So I could work for 1,000 years to be the best painter in the world and then never be exposed to art in their next life. What a rip off." I scoffed.

"Or on the contrary," Mkhail started, " when the moment is right in the next life, a paintbrush will fall into your hand, and what will be created will be so strangely natural and impeccable that the people around you will have no other choice than to feed the uniquely powerful talent. That's the thing about these Contracts. It creates something innately magnetizing that pulls opportunity towards you. The Energy never leaves your spirit. The fire of your efforts and an unspoken wisdom will remain. I know that you've always felt all your life that something was different. You couldn't explain what it was specifically, but you felt it in your heart all along."

How many times had I felt the ubiety
of a greying memory--
Lost in a time so distant from my own.
Visions too long ago to belong in my personal collection--
But too colourful and sharp to belong to anyone else.

"I could technically convince you to sign another Contract one day." He chuckled.
"Have I signed The Contract before?" I asked him.

He hesitated.

"Have I?!" I asked him again.
"Yes." He looked pleased.

I grabbed him by the shirt.

"How many times!?" I yelled.
"7." He smiled.

My stomach turned.

"There's no way."
"You ask me this every time!" He started laughing.
"So that means I have spent over 7,000 years with you??"

He was laughing so hard he was snorting like a wild boar.

"What were the reasons that I signed The Contract the last 7 times?" I bombarded him.
"I am not at liberty to say. It messes with the Grand Scheme of Things." He changed the subject--
"How would you like to have your hands back?" He asked me.

My eyes welled up with tears.

I thought about those lost, lonely dreams that I had put on the back burner.

Before I could answer his question--

Suddenly I was on a magnificent stage that resembled an old Opera Arena.

There was a colossal 100 ft. red Silk dangling down to the center of a dark hardwood floor.

The Silk seemed to beg for me to scale its length.

It cooed to me in the most lascivious fashion.

I heard Mkhail's voice in my ear.

"I am going to give you a taste of this power--

If you truly believe this is a dream--

Play along.

Show me how badly you want this.

Show me your flame.

Show me your madness.

Show me what the depths of misery resemble."

As the theater drapes parted open, they revealed a forbearing audience.

When my fingers touched the Silk--

I felt my blood surge with an acute electrical charge.

As I began to pull myself up off the ground there was no pain in my hands. I was stronger than I'd ever been before.

I climbed all the way to the top and looked down at all the tiny people waiting patiently for me astound them.

I began to wonder how many times I had done all of this before. How many talents had I acquired and wasted?

I thought about The Big Man.
What an asshole.

The estranged women of Le Cirque Maudit were standing in the shadows watching me closely.

I wondered what it would feel like to be totally free from all the insecurities that had ever held me back.

There had to be a way to do it on my own.
Even if I did find a way--
Mkhail could catch me at a moment of weakness and convince me to sign again.

I looked up into the night sky.
I could see the North Star.

The air was circulating around me.
I felt the planets start to align.

This was my only shot.

Then it dawned on me again—
None of this was real.

I spun down the Silk like a Thwaitesia Nigronodosa
descends from its web.
When--
I felt the presence of something far greater than my own mind
could comprehend.
There was a flash of light.

A melody began to play--
It was a song I hadn't heard in over 7,000 years.

I saw the Amazon rainforest.
I saw my 1st birthday party and my parents helping me blow
out the candles.
I saw grey skies, unfamiliar buildings and dark towers.
I saw myself as an old woman lying in a bed of Roses.
I saw the ancient pyramids reaching up to the Heavens.

Every truth I had built my foundation upon
quickly melted through my fingertips
back into the Earth.
I heard someone whisper my name,
except it was a name I was hearing for the first time.
Somehow,
I knew it had belonged to me before--

Before all this nonsense.

Follow me on Instagram! @Estranged.Behaviour

Send me an e-mail! <u>Estranged.Behaviour@gmail.com</u>

Friend me on Facebook:Facebook.com/Estranged.Lady